The Transreal

Political Aesthetics of Crossing Realities

Micha Cárdenas

Elle Mehrmand

Amy Sara Carroll

Ricardo Dominguez

Brian Holmes

James Morgan

Allucquére Rosanne Stone

Stelarc

Edited by Zach Blas and Wolfgang Schirmacher

Atropos Press

A version of "virus.circus.mem" was previously published in *SPECULATIVE*, by Lulu.com press.

A version of "Technésexual Interface" was previously published by Digimag, http://digicult.it.

For my Mom, Judith Cárdenas,
who never had a choice in being transreal

CONTENTS

Reality is Aesthetic and Political: Editor's Preface

Zach Blas

The Transreal arrives amidst a whirlwind of renewed philosophical interest in realism. Notably, the popularity of speculative realism has spun out across blogs, books, collected anthologies, and Facebook posts. This so-called philosophical turn has taken up not only realism and reality but also proffered critiques of worlding, materiality, and the subject. Although it might seem off-topic to begin this preface by engaging with speculative realism, its growing body of theoretical and cultural production--which now includes self-identified speculative realist artists--is an unavoidable interlocutor for this book. Crucially, Micha Cárdenas delivers an implicit refutation of speculative realism's "reality" in the following pages.

Speculative realism, a rapidly developing philosophical movement, argues for an ability to *speculatively* access that which exists beyond or outside the correlation of being and world. Notably, Quentin Meillassoux has referred to this as gaining access to "the great outdoors,"[1] while others simply refer to the reality they are after as a world without us.[2] Speculative realists posit that a world exists without humans, a world or reality that exceeds the perceptual world of the human, and

---

[1] Quentin Meillassoux, *After Finitude: An Essay on the Necessity of Contingency* (London: Continuum, 2008), 7.
[2] See Ray Brassier, Graham Harmon, Iain Hamilton Grant, Quentin Meillassoux, "Speculative Realism," *Collapse: Philosophical Research and Development Vol. III* (Urbanomic, 2007).

various techniques must be generated to gain access to such a world. For example, Meillassoux uses mathematics, while others like Reza Negarestani create extremist, para-academic, theoretical-fictions.[3] Importantly, there is an aesthetic dimension to these texts: speculative realism for Meillassoux is "the glacial world"[4] and for Negarestani it is a fiery oil apocalypse filled with charred, blackened corpses. Others interlocutors, like Dominic Fox, offer an aesthetics of black metal, gloom, and coldness.[5] In object-oriented philosophy (OOP), a strand of speculative realism, Graham Harman gives us an aesthetics of lists[6] and also claims that aesthetics is first-philosophy, not ethics as Emmanuel Levinas previously suggested,[7] but his prioritization of aesthetics evacuates the human at the expense of an apolitical choreography of objects.

When we consider the aesthetic and political realisms and realities of speculative realism--and they are all *aesthetic and political*--we find ourselves placed within a particular configuration of coldness and human absence or disintegration.

---

[3] See Reza Negarestani, *Cyclonopedia: Complicity with Anonymous Materials* (Melbourne: re.press, 2008).

[4] Meillassoux, 115.

[5] See Dominic Fox, *Cold World: The Aesthetics of Dejection and the Politics of Militant Dysphoria* (UK: Zero Books, 2009).

[6] Such as "pollen, oxygen, eagles, or windmills." See Graham Harman, *Guerrilla Metaphysics: Phenomenology and the Carpentry of Things* (Chicago: Open Court, 2005), 1.

[7] See Graham Harman, "Aesthetics as First Philosophy: Levinas and the Non-Human," *Naked Punch* Issue 9 (Summer/Fall 2007).

Yet, as much as these thinkers might wish to do away with or destroy the human body and human concerns, their realities are always already culturally parsed through class, gender, and race. Although many of these texts have been criticized for their lack of political engagement, there initially were calls to seek, discover, and excavate the political dimension.[8] There were even attempts at object-oriented feminisms,[9] but these gestures fell prey to that dreaded correlationist trap that keeps human subjectivity at play in the constitution or identification of an object or reality. Now, attention to the political problem of speculative realism has dwindled with no sufficiently posited possibilities, let alone answers. Perhaps these failures suggest that the political can never be adequately addressed through this framework, or more insidiously, the framework encourages evasion of the political.

If we take notice that most speculative realist writers are white, heterosexual men, then it might not be a far stretch to state that the reality in speculative realism is a privilege and luxury to think and study. Their writings dictate a reality indifferent to various marginalized struggles of the everyday, to

---

[8] See Nathan Brown, "On *After Finitude*: A Response to Peter Hallward," *Speculative Heresy* Blog (November 2008), http://speculativeheresy.wordpress.com/2008/11/16/on-after-finitude-a-response-to-peter-hallward

[9] See the program for the 2010 Society for Literature, Science, and the Arts Conference, http://www.litsciarts.org/slsa10/program.php

sexual and racial violence, to the dirty political battles that
constitute the realities and realisms of the queer, the
transgendered, the persons of color. The question becomes what
are one's ethical and political obligations when writing and
constructing a conception of reality and realism? If one of the
major trends in contemporary philosophy and critical thought
today is the construction of a reality that abandons these political
concerns, Cárdenas transports us to another "outdoors," another
speculative reality.

The implicit critique of speculative realism in *The Transreal*
goes like this: If Meillassoux's outdoors is only attainable in
mathematics, who would actually desire this realism? If
Negarestani's radical openness is "catastrophically unpleasant"[10]
for the human subject, who would desire it? Why is the world
without us aesheticized as such? Why isn't it exuberant,
superabundant, affirmatively chaotic--even if it is without us?
The realities of speculative realism are what Hakim Bey once
called Intellectual S/M, which is the intellectualized and fascist
drive toward death and mutilation.[11] Do the writers of

---

[10] Negarestani, 200.

[11] See Hakim Bey's "Communique #5: Intellectual S/M is the
Fascism of the EIghties--The Avant-Garde Eats Shit and Likes
It" from *T.A.Z.: The Temporary Autonomous Zone* (New York:
Autonomedia, 2003). Bey writes, "Self-mutilating 'performance'
artists strike us as banal & stupid--their art makes everyone *more
unhappy*. What kind of two-bit conniving horseshit...what kind
of cockroach-brained Art creeps cooked up this apocalypse
stew? [...] Compared to that kind of intelligence we'd choose real

speculative realism conjure such horrors as a way to indulge in that which they will probably never experience, namely, the violence and destruction against minoritarian populations? Just as OOP's objects forever withdraw from the world, so do most of these philosophers' political concerns for the present moment, which is a world with humans and nonhumans. While both have an investment in the speculative and the real, *The Transreal* demonstrates that speculative realism is not yet compatible with a queer and transgendered politics.[12]

The Transreal aligns with another trajectory of the speculative, as those creative forces that generate utopic ideality to change what is real. The transreal dimension of the speculative partners with José Esteban Muñoz's queer futurity and Samuel R. Delany's queer science fictions.[13] These works

---

stupidity, bucolic New Age blissed-out inanity--we'd rather be pinheads than *queer for death*. [...] Ours is no art of mutilation but of excess, superabundance, amazement."

[12] It is important to note, however, that Michael O'Rourke is courageously and carefully attempting to articulate a queer speculative realism. See his article "'Girls Welcome!!!' Speculative Realism, Object Oriented Ontology and Queer Theory" in *Speculations II*.

[13] For this queer speculative perspective, see José Esteban Muñoz, *Cruising Utopia: The Then and There of Queer Futurity* (New York: New York University Press, 2009); Zach Blas and Christopher O'Leary, editors, *Speculative* (Los Angeles Contemporary Exhibitions, 2011, featuring the writing of Micha Cárdenas and collaborator Elle Mehrmand); and Jayna Brown and Alexis Lothian, "Speculative Life: Introduction," *Social Text Periscope* (January 2012),

posit a politics of the speculative that states we do not yet know what reality is or can be, so we must ethically and politically invest our imaginations into creating and experimenting with the realities we desire.

As no surprise, Cárdenas' reality ends up inherently different from the speculative realist version because it affirms and is powerfully invested in politics, ethics, a human subject, and the abilities of the imagination to produce multiple realities. Furthermore, *The Transreal* does not even define reality but presents various cases and examples of what it can and might be from Cardenas' and other artists' practices. There is a political motivation to leave reality open, an understanding that it can, should, must be left open as a tactic necessary for survival. As the Zapatistas say, "In the world we want, many worlds to fit."[14]

Speculative realists might engage with the nonhuman at the expense of the human, but the transreal accommodates both. The crucial point is not that the transreal invests in an older formation of identity politics with the human firmly at its center, while speculative realism expands into the cosmological. *The*

---

http://www.socialtextjournal.org/periscope/2012/01/speculative-life-introduction.php

[14] EZLN, "Fourth Declaration From the Lacandón Jungle," *The Zapatista Reader* (New York: Thunder's Mouth Press, 2001), 250. The original Spanish is "El mundo que queremos es uno donde quepan muchos mundos".

Transreal aligns with a body of work that explores the nonhuman in queer contexts.[15] For Cárdenas, the human is anything but stable and centralized; consider her projects on becoming-animal, techné-sexual, and viruses as instances of non/human transformation. Cárdenas pursues worlds and perspectives that are other than human; yet, she creates with care and compassion toward those that have always been cast out of the normatively human world.

Cárdenas also writes of her own uses of various technologies, including virtual and immersive reality systems, and even provides the computer code used during a performance. This direct, practical engagement with nonhuman materials directly comes to bear on Cárdenas' theory of the transreal. Perhaps this is the major difference between speculative realists and Cárdenas: hers is a lived, practiced concept, concerned with a mode of living rather than solely an academic conversation or contribution. Hers is a praxis which, in fact, the book itself is an active part of, just as her artworks, performances, installations, and talks are. We have yet to see the speculative realists put their philosophy into a practice of everyday life, partially because this is impossible but also because it is not their concern.

The Transreal argues that if we only want to *think* reality, maybe we should turn to the speculative realists or search for

---

[15] See Noreen Giffney and Myra J. Hird, editors, *Queering the Non/Human* (Aldershot, England: Ashgate, 2008).

any other academic conception of reality that allows the human body to withdraw from intellectual concern. However, if we want to *think and live* reality, change reality, embody it, fight exploitation and violence, and discover its astounding, incredible, multiple dimensions, then participating in the aesthetic and political construction of making realities that are human and beyond is a promising and empowering practice that can make life livable and joyfully intensified. Existing as transreal teaches us that to produce an artistic or philosophical project that imagines or theorizes into existence a world without us is a privilege that many queer and transgendered people cannot afford to invest in as they struggle to exist in a world that is painfully and amazingly present. Cárdenas' realities are lived diagrams of transreal existence, and as such, they are inspired and needed framings of realities that have, can, and will be.

Acknowledgements

Throughout the development of this work and the ideas that drive it, Ricardo Dominguez has been a major inspiration and dedicated friend and mentor to me, for which I will endlessly be grateful. Amy Sara Carroll provided me with both invaluable editing and thinking suggestions for the poems in *Becoming Transreal* and *Becoming Dragon* and has also been a continuing inspiration as a poet and loving friend in the time when this book was written.

Becoming Dragon received support from the Center for Research in Computing and the Arts at UCSD (CRCA), Ars Virtua and the California Institute for Telecommunications and Information Technology. Throughout the development of these projects, both my solo work and my collaborations with Elle Mehrmand have been generously supported by the University of California Institute for Research in the Arts (UCIRA). I owe a huge debt of gratitude to CRCA, not only for providing financial support but also for providing my work with a physical home and continued nourishment thanks to the hard work of Sheldon Brown, Todd Margolis, Lourdes Guardiano-Durkin and Helena Bristow. *Becoming Transreal* was created thanks to the support of the UCLA Center for Performance Studies and CRCA, along with the UCLA Department of Theater, LGBT Studies, the Center for the Study of Women and the Center for Research in Engineering, Media and Performance (REMAP).

Numerous people helped move this book from an archive of videos and texts to a book and I am deeply grateful to all of them. Two students of the European Graduate School helped with the panel transcriptions: Trista di Genova and Jennifer Hsu. Additionally, Jessica Leaman provided her brilliant and dilligent copy editing talent. Hannes Charen of Atropos Press was my continued line of communication and support throughout the process, for which I am very grateful. Wolfgang Schirmacher at Atropos Press deserves much gratitude for being an enthusiastic supporter of my scholarship as well as an intellectual inspiration as an unflinching iconoclast and trouble maker.

I am so profoundly grateful to my former partner, collaborator and lover Elle Mehrmand for her daily love and femme disturbance beauty, strength, passionate allyship, laughter and brilliant collaboration during the writing of much of this book.

As an editor, intellectual peer and perhaps my best friend, I am so deeply indebted to Zach Blas. Zach showed a continued commitment to this project and helped me more than anyone else to see it to fruition. No other artist/theorist in the world holds as much resonance for my own thinking as Zach Blas.

In the last few weeks of the writing and editing of this book, Claire Elise Morey has brought me indescribable happiness and joy. It is amazing to me how much one's conception of reality and possibility can be so transformed in such a short time by the love of another person.

Introduction

In Fall 2004, a senior aide to George W. Bush said in an interview with the New York Times Magazine, "We're an empire now, and when we act, we create our own reality. And while you're studying that reality—judiciously, as you will—we'll act again, creating other new realities… We're history's actors…and you, all of you, will be left to just study what we do."[16] The aide was later identified as Karl Rove.[17] After ignoring the largest protests against a war in world history on February 15, 2003, the Bush administration now made clear with these words what its political strategy really was. At the time, I was dedicating much of my life, including going to jail, in order to stop the wars in Iraq and Afghanistan, and these words struck me as beyond audacious; they seemed to offer a rare illuminated glimpse in media coverage of the grim political situation of the day. I recall them now to illustrate the broad significance of the concepts I am proposing in this book. While the writing here will examine methods that contemporary artists are using to create and manipulate realities, the goal is not merely to

---

[16] Ron Suskind, "Faith, Certainty and the Presidency of George W. Bush," *The New York Times*, October 17, 2004, sec. Magazine, http://www.nytimes.com/2004/10/17/magazine/17BUSH.html.
[17] Mark Danner, "Words in a Time of War: On Rhetoric, Truth and Power," in Andras Szanto and Orville Schell, *What Orwell Didn't Know: Propaganda and the New Face of American Politics*, Reprint. (PublicAffairs, 2007).

explicate the fine details of an avant-garde art practice aimed at an insular audience of art scholars and practitioners. In today's transmedia environment, we see a proliferation of forms of mixed reality, including augmented reality advertising from BMW and alternate reality games such as Jane McGonigal's EVOKE, funded by the World Bank[18]. The goal is to learn from contemporary artists' work in developing avant-garde forms of media in order to be able to more effectively critique and find political agency in a world whose ground seems to be constantly shifting and being redefined by the likes of Karl Rove and major corporations. The goal is ultimately to be able not only to respond to the changing shape of reality, but to initiate change as well.

The Transreal: Political Aesthetics of Crossing Realities is a book that explores the use of multiple realities as a medium in contemporary art. Building on the notion of "trans" from "transgender," I propose that transreal aesthetics cross the boundaries of realities created by a fragmentation of reality that occurred as a result of postmodern theory and emerging technologies. Queer theorist Jack Halberstam informs the concept of the transreal by making "the perhaps overly ambitious claim that there is such a thing as 'queer time' and

---

[18] http://blog.urgentevoke.net/2010/01/27/about-the-evoke-game/

'queer space.'"[19] Expanding on this, one can see the acceptance of multiple worlds, times, and realities as a fundamental characteristic of late postmodernism or post-postmodernism. While Fredric Jameson has claimed that late postmodernism is characterized by a return to the real, I argue that such a return is impossible. In contrast, thinkers such as Halberstam, Dipesh Chakrabarty and Gilles Deleuze propose a multiplicity of times and spaces which coexist. From there, one can look at contemporary artists' attempts to create and work with realities as a similar form of multiplicity. Building on the notion of experimental affective politics that I developed in my first book, *Trans Desire/Affective Cyborgs*, co-authored with Barbara Fornssler, I claim that an understanding of building and working with multiple realities is essential for artists and political actors who wish to be effective in a post-contemporary field of proliferating realities.

Instead of offering a definition of reality, defining being an act that may limit possibilities, I hope to identify operations and operators that can make connections and create resonances. My work is not driven towards a perhaps phallocentric mode of proving an argument, but a mode described by Colectivo Situaciones as "more as a search for

---

[19] Judith Halberstam, *In a Queer Time and Place: Transgender Bodies, Subcultural Lives* (New York: New York University Press, 2005), 1.

(producing-receiving) resonances than as a transmission of messages."[20] Combining elements of multiple methodologies including media studies, performance studies and queer and gender studies, my approach is mixed, similar to what Fatima El-Tayeb describes as a "creolization of theory."[21]

My hope is that in lieu of a definition of reality, this book will give the reader an understanding of different artists' attempts to work with and create realities and thus give a sense of their contours and workings. The question of reality is one of the oldest questions in philosophy; one could look to Plato's allegory of the cave, for example. My own working definition of reality is related to the definitions set forth by a number of theorists. Heidegger's sense of world is related to the notion of reality, but because it relies on a specific *Gestell*, or framework for being-in-the-world, such as the combination of human bodies with the particular qualities of gravity, air and light that enable both movement and perception, its scale seems smaller than that of a reality. In contrast, Gilles Deleuze's notion of a plane, such as the plane of the virtual or the plane of immanence, is closer to

---

[20] Colectivo Situaciones, "Something More on Research Militancy: Footnotes on Procedures and (In)Decisions," in *Constituent imagination: militant investigations//collective theorization,* ed. Stevphen Shukaitis et al., (AK Press, 2007), 91.
[21] Fatima El-Tayeb, *European Others: Queering Ethnicity in Postnational Europe* (Univ Of Minnesota Press, 2011), xxxvii.

the scale of what I imagine a reality to be, but is missing elements of reality created by the experience of being human. Rather than use the oppositional logic of Jean Baudrillard's "neither real, nor unreal: hyperreal," [22] the transreal is more akin to a Derridean both/and, both real and unreal at the same time.

A reality must include both a *Gestell*, or framework that provides a space, and a human interaction with that space. The notion of the real in psychoanalysis begins to get at this when Jacques Lacan, describing the Freudian conception of desire, refers to "the Other as reality."[23] Jack Halberstam's concepts of time and space are perhaps the closest to my understanding of reality in that they involve an interaction between an existing ontological situation and an individual desire or agency that shapes perception, because queer time is shaped by the choice of individuals to eschew a heteronormative life narrative of marrying and producing children. Queer theory is useful also for making a link to another definition of reality, as when Lauren Berlant and Michael Warner say, "By queer culture we mean a world-making project, where 'world,' like 'public,' differs from community or group because it necessarily includes more people than can be identified, more spaces than can be mapped

---

[22] Jean Baudrillard, *Simulacra and Simulation* (University of Michigan Press, 1995), 125.

[23] Jacques Lacan, *Ecrits: A Selection* (W. W. Norton & Company, 2004), 287.

beyond a few reference points, modes of feeling that can be learned rather than experienced as a birthright."[24] These theories of worlds, spaces, and times take on new meaning when applied to specific examples such as the virtual reality technologies that later led to the development of mixed and alternate reality games and art.

The characteristics that define virtual reality can serve as a useful guidepost here before we establish more complex operations that create mixed and augmented realities. Historically, virtual reality has been characterized by four elements:

- *the visual (and aural and haptic) displays that immerse the user in the virtual world and that block out contradictory sensory impressions from the real world;*

- *the graphics rendering system that generates, at 20 to 30 frames per second, ever-changing images;*

- *the tracking system that continually reports the position and orientation of the user's head and limbs; and*

---

[24] Lauren Berlant and Michael Warner, "Sex in Public," in *Publics and Counterpublics*, Michael Warner, (Zone, 2005).

> • *the database construction and maintenance system for*
>   *building and maintaining detailed and realistic models*
>   *of the virtual world.*[25]

There is a similarity here between queer theorists' conceptions of worlds, times, and spaces and the more technical definitions of virtual reality. Both Berlant and Warner's notion of a world being something that is too large to know and Halberstam's notion of time and space being shaped by agency can help build a conception of how believability works in virtual reality environments as both an enabling and shaping force. A reality is something that limits and enables action but also takes its shape through belief. The artists and projects discussed in this book work in different ways to attempt to create believability, through narrative, visual illusion, and usage of gestures which have an accepted meaning but can be shifted slightly to mean something else. Still, as these artists attempt to go beyond a single reality to blending multiple realities, there is always an element of play with believability rather than a rigid attempt to establish a perfectly seamless reality.

The transreal slips. Existing in multiple realities, transreal gestures tumble, shift, and fall through different locations and meanings without moving. Emerging out of

---

[25] F.P. Brooks, Jr., "What's Real About Virtual Reality?" *IEEE Computer Graphics and Applications* 19(1999): 16-27.

thinking about my experience as a transgender woman and the intersections of gender and contemporary networked technology, I created the concept transreal. Working with Ricardo Dominguez for years to bring together data bodies and physical bodies to create political disturbances to power structures of capital, war and immigration, after co-organizing virtual sit-ins and codeveloping the *Transborder Immigrant Tool*, I sought to create a word to describe my practice of Mixed Reality Performance Art. The transreal emerged from a feeling of political urgency in a time of war, economic collapse, the contemporary slavery of the Prison Industrial Complex and daily violence against people around the world, and a desperate urge to find new forms of political action able to address the biopolitics of gender and infiltrate digital networks of communication. Reflecting on this notion of transreal now, I will attempt to evoke some of its possible ramifications and its specificities. One can consider the transreality of a medium such as writing, as it brings together the present moment of my authoring these words with a future moment of you, the reader, performing the words in your mind and bringing them to life. Yet one can also see in contemporary art a number of gestures that can be said to be more intentionally transreal.

The transreal emerged as a response to the daily experience, with varying degrees of violence or banality, of being told that as a queer femme transgender woman my gender was not real, my sexuality was not real and even my body was not real. At times this critique came viciously from so-called feminists who didn't share my vision of what feminism could mean, and it continues to happen on a daily basis in my interactions with people who want to tell me that I am a man. The transreal is the embracing of an identity that is a combination of my "real" body that I was born with and my personal history with another identity that I have written in flesh, in words, in pixels, in 3-dimensional models and across multiple strata of communications technologies. To say that I am transreal is a strategy for embracing a gender that exceeds daily reality on Planet Earth and that says back to all the people who have tried to make me choose between man or woman that I choose to be a shape-shifter, a dragon and a light wave.

Many contemporary artists, such as Blast Theory, Mez Breeze, Reza Negarestani, and myself in collaboration with Elle Mehrmand, create artworks that demonstrate what I have termed the transreal: crossing boundaries of multiple realities, a nuance for a multiplicity of worlds and the usage of reality as a medium. In contrast to contributing to the very widespread attention paid to the latest augmented reality technologies from smartphone ads to technology blogs to music videos employing tropes of augmented interfaces, I will focus on the specific operations that artists are using for allowing viewer/participants to enter into realities. These artists focus less on the illusion of realistic graphics or immersive visual interfaces and more on what has been described as "social immersion".[26]

Transrealities, Explicit Reality Construction

Perhaps the most well known artist group working on mixed reality games today is Blast Theory, whose work has spanned from fully immersive virtual reality installations, to a lottery where one can win the prize of being kidnapped, to games delivered through a variety of mobile technology platforms. Blast Theory's most recent work, *Ulrike and Eamon Compliant (UEC)*, created in collaboration with the Mixed Reality Lab at the University of Nottingham and exhibited at the 2009 Venice Biennale, sees the group, as they describe it, returning to more directly political themes and employing voice, video and live action performances as a means to immersing the audience/participant in the life of one of two well-known leftist militants, Eamon Collins and Ulrike Meinhof. I will focus here on the group's attitudes toward the idea of reality and on the notion of believability expressed by participants, as it applies to the politics of the performance *UEC*.

Ulrike and Eamon Compliant sees Blast Theory returning to the direct political engagement of earlier works,

---

[26] Tom Boellstorff, *Coming of Age in Second Life: An Anthropologist Explores the Virtually Human* (Princeton University Press, 2010), 116.

including *Desert Rain* and *Kidnap*. It is a locative media project that engages the participants in a walk, using a mobile phone to speak to them as though they are each either Ulrike Meinhoff or Eamon Collins. Like the *Transborder Immigrant Tool*, a locative media project I have worked on that deals with the US/Mexico Border, *UEC* relies on a low-tech approach to mixed reality. Blast Theory artists describe their idea of alternate reality gaming by saying "for an artwork to be successful it needs to posit an alternate reality in some way, it needs to draw you into a new terrain where slightly different codes might be at work . . . it creates a new world but at the same time enables you to see the real world through a new lens."[27] For Blast Theory, the immersion that the participant feels matches up with the idea of social immersion that Salen and Zimmerman proposed in *Rules of Engagement.* They describe the "Immersive Fallacy" that immersion in games is created through illusion and propose instead that immersion "is an engagement that occurs through play itself," an interactive and often social experience.[28] The artists of Blast Theory are primarily concerned with the emotional reaction to the experience of the characters, asking participants to imagine to "learn to shoot and to be shot at." Building on this affective level of immersion, Blast Theory

---

[27] "Ulrike and Eamon. Compliant," accessed January 5, 2012, http://www.dlwp.com/dlwpinternational/venice/index.html#.
[28] Katie Salen and Eric Zimmerman, *Rules of Play: Game Design Fundamentals* (Cambridge, Mass.: MIT Press, 2004), 450.

expands "out to social and political realities," having the work culminate in a face-to-face discussion between the participants and the artists in a secret, hidden interrogation room. On the group's website participants describe the experience as ""Surreal … scary… unnerving…," "powerful" and a "displacement."[29] Their comments seem to meet the goals of Blast Theory, whose members hope that "the experience creates a parallel and, at times, unnerving reality to the physical world through which you are walking."[30] Through *UEC*, one can see the intentional creation of an alternate reality as a strategy for building political empathy and experimentation in an audience for art. Many of the participants in the project relate their experience in the work back to their political experiences, but perhaps the effectiveness of the work is best summarized by one participant who says, "I didn't expect such a deep-going experience in this snobby surrounding. For me it was a complete new form of artwork and I am surprised how much it touched me — I even feel like art could be able to change things. So in a way it give me back something I lost years ago."[31] [sic]

My own works in collaboration with Elle Mehrmand, *Becoming Transreal* and *virus.circus*, are our most

---

[29] "Ulrike and Eamon. Compliant," accessed January 5, 2012, http://www.dlwp.com/dlwpinternational/venice/index.html#.
[30] Ibid.
[31] Ibid.

direct attempts to use a similar strategy of bringing the audience into an alternate reality.

Becoming Transreal (2010) was performed at the UCLA Freud Playhouse and consisted of a ritual in which I would read a poem, and once the poem ended, Elle Mehrmand would use a hand pump to increase the pressure in suction cups attached to my breasts. In this one-hour performance, I wore a head-mounted display, and both Elle and I were motion-captured by a Vicon motion capture system that moved our avatar's positions in the world based on our positions in the real physical performance space. Throughout, Elle Mehrmand performed live music and sang in English and Farsi. The narrative of *Becoming Transreal* implicates the audience directly by describing a future reality in which audiences pay to feel performers' motion captured movements, while the real audience views the motion captured performance in stereoscopic 3-D, with motion capture cameras on stage and Second Life avatars animated by the data projected behind the performers. The slipstream poetry of *Becoming Transreal* is based on my experience of transitioning physically as a result of administered hormones and the support I was so generously given by my partner Elle, but imagines those experiences through a narrative of future nano-bio drug production inside the patient's body, drug piracy and transnational migration experiences. Chapters in the book about *Becoming Transreal* include the poems from the performance as well as the transcript of the panel discussion after the performance with Allucquére Rosanne (Sandy) Stone, Ricardo Dominguez and Amy Sara Carroll.

Another of my works with Elle Mehrmand, *virus.circus* (2010—2011), follows the viral as a transversal line of inquiry that intersects with the militarization of medical authority, microscopic transnational migrations and global economic inequality. Consisting of an episodic series of performances using wearable electronics, soft sensors and live audio to bridge virtual and physical spaces, the performances explore queer futures of latex sexuality and DIY medicine amidst a speculative world of virus hysteria. The history of queer politics shows that the rhetoric of viruses such as HIV is used to control marginalized populations, while viruses such as H1N1 reproduce these structures of power. Code switching between mixed and alternate reality, *virus.circus* asks how we can use reality as a medium, resonating across a number of modes including public space interventions, performances in museums and galleries and networked performances. Wearable sensors allow the performers to experiment with transreal embodiment, performing with their physical bodies and Second Life avatars simultaneously.

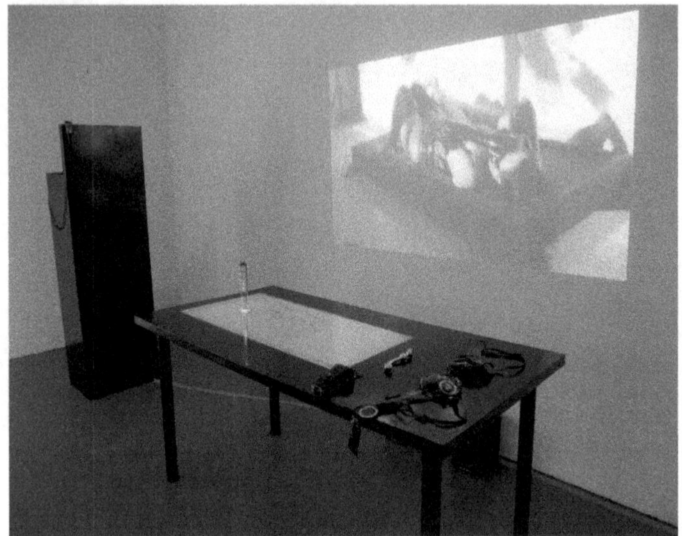

virus.circus.mem (2011), Los Angeles Contemporary Exhibitions,
Speculative Exhibition, Photo: Christopher O'Leary

    virus.circus.mem, pictured here, involves an imaginary
computational system that needs lube, semen and female
ejaculate fliud to operate. The system imagines biometric and
visual recordings that are replayed through a direct neocortical
interface that has the ability to "play back" memories as if they
were real experiences. In order to immerse the viewer in this
experience, the installation of the work at the Los Angeles
Contemporary Exhibitions gallery included a 3D stereoscopic
screen displaying an augmented reality view of a real physical
table on display in the gallery. Viewers entering the gallery
would see the table with props on it and a glowing animated
display of biometric data scrolling across it, with videos of

performances projected on the wall above it. To the left of the table stood a pedestal with a screen obscured from view of people standing at the table. Moving in front of the pedestal, viewers are presented with an augmented view of the table with the same props and from the same angle, but with Mehrmand and Cárdenas standing on either side of the table. As the augmented video proceeds, the performers use the computational interface of the table, involving sexual acts with the props on the table, and proceed to masturbate, perhaps providing the interface with the necessary input or perhaps experiencing a relived memory through the device. The viewer is left to fill in the reasons for specific acts.

Transreal Performativity, Transreal Identities

The work of Mary-Anne (Mez) Breeze uses linguistic and typographic conventions from programming languages and networked social spaces to achieve what she refers to as "reality_flexing,"[32] rejecting boundaries of genre, profession and identity with every word. Mez, who has many pseudonyms, invents genres of writing and coding and her work has been written about in many different contexts. To attempt any comprehensive explanation of the complex enfolding of spaces, ideas and characters in these works seems futile. Instead, I will

---

[32] "Re:Interview #005: Versatile m[c]o[mmunication]dality | Mary-Anne Breeze | CONT3XT.NET", accessed January 5, 2012, http://cont3xt.net/blog/?p=251.

discuss Mez's stated goals of creating and flexing realities and show the many-layered performativity of multiple simultaneous charavatars in a few of her codeworks.

The code poetry of Mez is aimed at "reality_flexing." Deeply commited to an iconoclastic method, she is not interested in entering accepted realms but in creating entirely new ones. In an interview she describes her process with this line of poetry:

#boundaries = accept[raditi(can)on(ic)al]ed definiti[c]on[ception]s of wot comprises knowledge.[33]

Later she says that she is "concentrating more on a type of reality_flexing than substant[rad]i[c]ally altering established disciplines."[34]

One of the primary methods through which Mez does this is an experimental writing practice of performing "_charavatars_,"[35] related to the performativity of writers including "#kathy acker,"[36] whom she lists as an inspiration. This performance of multiple identities includes as a key component "the willing suspension of disbelief required 4 seamless avatar adoption rather than the mainstream ideal of

---

[33] "Re:Interview #005: Versatile m[c]o[mmunication]dality | Mary-Anne Breeze | CONT3XT.NET"
[34] Ibid.
[35] Ibid.
[36] Ibid.

avatar-as-basic-ego-projection via a similar geo-physical|psychological skin."[37] Through these multiple performances, Mez often explores questions of gender. The literary technique she has developed is called Mezangelle, but she has also developed other "synthetic_genre[s]" such as "_[twitte]reality_fictions_."[38] In her writing for the Version micro-journal entitled ".[S/PACE_98 = [TWITTE]REALITY_FICTIONS_09].061609" she writes:

[ponderin:gender-loads+pedag(l)ogical>instructional vs ego-pinched arrogance:

"Identities in this mirror are Spock-ier than they appear"][39]

The performance of multiple realities in Mez's work resonates with one of the original experiences I had that led me to the concept of the transreal. As a transgender person, I am aware of the slipperiness and multiplicity of the moment of passing in which someone's perception of one's gender can shift back and forth rapidly, like a kind of shimmering mirage, or can be multiple and incongruous. Mez's writing for the Critical Code Studies working group engaged directly with the intersections of gender and technology, raising questions about mastery over

---

[37] "Re:Interview #005: Versatile m[c]o[mmunication]dality | Mary-Anne Breeze | CONT3XT.NET"
[38] "v.content", accessed January 5, 2012, http://version.org/textuals/12.
[39] "v.content"

technology as the only possible relationship to technology and assumptions about programming skill based on people's gender at birth.

```
################################################
##########
```

```
#[-d](pre)face: OOPs. this is buggy_as_all_hell.
pls fix?
```

```
################################################
##########
```

```
...
```

```
#[read:] I'm.A.Great.Big.Code[r].[im]Pos[t]er#
```

```
+...s[eek(ing)2]tr[ing]etch.ing.conventions.beyo
nd.[pro]grammatical.boundaries
#I.Suffer.[From].Systematic.SocialWare[-
z].In[Trans| ]clusion#
```

```
...
```

```
+m[ez]angelled_[wo]manipulation_eg:
```
[40]

With these lines, Mez uses Mezangelle to literally link femaleness with manipulation, underscoring both the assumption that femininity is intended to manipulate its viewer and the

---

[40] "Week 6 - Critical Code Studies Working Group", accessed January 5, 2012, http://critcode.ning.com/forum/topics/week-6.

ability of women to manipulate source code. One can read the
above lines as a self-deprecating admission of a lack of mastery
but also as a clever subversion of the drive for mastery. She
describes her drive here as seeking to exceed the boundaries of
the programmatic, both in terms of literal functionality and in
terms of commonly assigned gender roles in technology, striving
not for inclusion but instead for trans-clusion.

While much of Mez's writing has borrowed
conventions from online communities such as 4chan, often
associated with the online hacktivist group Anonymous, her
most recent works deal directly with the performativity and
politics of Anonymous and LulzSec. Since the group
Anonymous is composed of a literally anonymous global
network of hackers, describing them selves as "legion"[41] and as
having "no official messages… no official videos,"[42] "united as
one, divided by zero,"[43] Mez's performativity of multiple
characters is particularly apt. In works such as "[-eat-these-
delicious-rebellion(_Lulz_B)oats-]," Mez writes:

---

[41] "Message to Scientology - YouTube", accessed January 5,
2012,
http://www.youtube.com/watch?v=JCbKv9yiLiQ&feature=chan
nel_video_title.
[42] "Message to Anonymous - YouTube", accessed January 5,
2012, http://www.youtube.com/watch?v=_N3azFf6wiY.
[43] "Who is Anonymous? - YouTube", accessed January 5, 2012,
http://www.youtube.com/watch?v=2K0E8sMDJ9M.

```
_There's-A-Definite_LuL_In-Established-
Conve(ntional)RS(S.oblig)aT(ory)ional-F(BI)Low_
_U-th(RT)Ink-Mid-East-Riot_(sic{k})bags::We(t)-
Breath-(fl)Utter(ed)-CoR(I)PoRate+Rot+SPew_


:


:Lulzsec[ondary+Anon_1st]:[44]
```

With this work about Anonymous and Lulzsec, she explores the implications of performing a character of pure multiplicity, with no identity and an infinite number of identities. At times the reader wonders if Mez participates in this anonymous network or is an onlooker fascinated with its power to bring down corporations, take out government websites and threaten national sovereignties. Here the transreal can be seen in the performativity of an identity that creates its own realities and constantly shifts between them, avoiding detection and control through its undefinability and imperceptibility.

In *Becoming Dragon* (2008) I performed multiple simultaneous characters across multiple realities, including being a transgender performance artist available to a public in real physical space and a dragon avatar in Second Life. *Becoming Dragon* questions the one-year requirement of "Real

---

[44] "netwurker: [-eat-these-delicious-rebellion(_Lulz_B)oats-]", accessed January 5, 2012, http://netwurker.livejournal.com/132340.html.

Life Experience" that transgender people must fulfill in order to receive Gender Confirmation Surgery, and asks if this could be replaced by one year of "Second Life Experience" to lead to Species Reassignment Surgery. For the performance, I lived for 365 hours immersed in the online 3D environment of Second Life with a head-mounted display, seeing the physical world only through a video feed, and used a motion capture system to map my movements into Second Life. The installation included a stereoscopic projection for the audience. A Pure Data patch was used to process my voice to create a virtual dragon's voice. During the year of research and development of this project, I began my real-life hormone replacement therapy and wrote poetry and prose about the experience, which was included in the performance. The project was realized through a collaboration of myself, Christopher Head, Elle Mehrmand, Kael Greco, Ben Lotan and Anna Storelli. Chapters in the book about *Becoming Dragon* include a chapter of poems from the performance, source code used for the performance and transcriptions of public conversations with Stelarc on "The Body in Transmission/Transition: Learning to Live in Mixed Realities", with Allucquere Rosanne (Sandy) Stone on "Gender and Desire in Virtual Worlds" and with Brian Holmes and James Morgan on "Imagining New Worlds: Biopolitics and Self-Governance in Second Life."

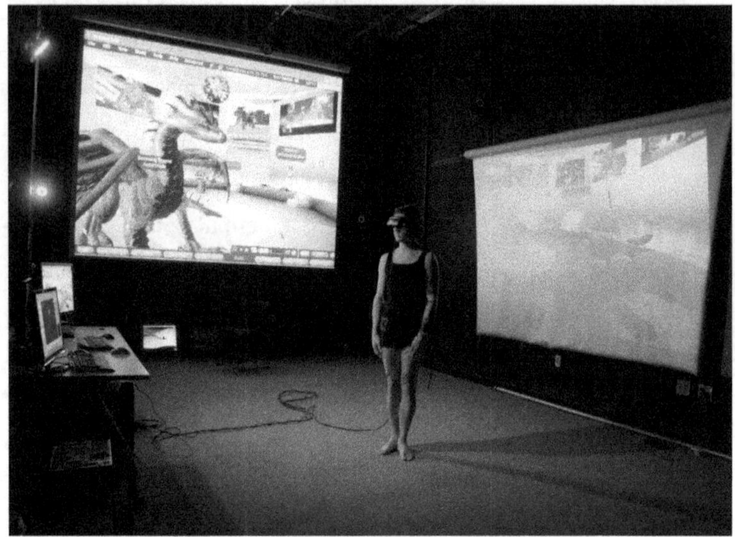

Becoming Dragon (2008) Installation view. Photo: Elle Mehrmand

Transreal Technologies: Imagining New Logics

The third operation for creating and dealing with multiple realities can be seen in the work of Ricardo Dominguez, Reza Negarestani and Zach Blas. All three of these artists have imagined trajectories of technology that bend truth values to exceed Western reason and invent their own logics.

At times described as the originator of the concept of Hacktivism, former member of Critical Art Ensemble and founder of Electronic Disturbance Theater Ricardo Dominguez developed a concept called Mayan Technology, which has been presented in performances including *Stories of Mayan*

Technology (2000), *Mayan Technology: Dia de los Muertes* (2002) and *Mayan Technology: A Polyspacial Tale* (2006). Dominguez's descriptions of Mayan Technology defy definition, so I will quote an interview with him here.

What is "Mayan Technology" and how does it relate to your work?

I will respond with a story from sub-comandante Marcos.

... The village is in assembly when a Commander-type plane, blue and yellow, from the Army Rainbow Task Force and a pinto helicopter from the Mexican Air Force, begin a series of low over flights above the community. The assembly does not stop; instead those who are speaking merely raise their voices. Pedrito is fed up with having the artillery aircraft above him, and he goes, fiercely, in search of a stick inside his hut. Pedrito comes out of his house with a piece of wood, and he angrily declares that "I'm going to hit the airplane because it's bothering me a lot." I smile to myself at the child's ingenuousness.

The plane makes a pass over Pedrito's hut, and he raises the stick and waves it furiously at the war plane. The plane then changes its course and leaves in the direction of its base. ...

Without saying anything else, we take it with us. We run into Tacho as we're leaving. "And that?" he asks, pointing to Pedrito's stick which we had taken. "Mayan technology," the Sea responds.

Trying to remember what Pedrito did I swing at the air with the stick. Suddenly the helicopter turned into a useless tin vulture, and the sky became golden and the clouds floated by like marzipan.

EDT and FloodNet are an example of Mayan technology. A stick that crosses the boundaries of what it is and becomes the unbearable weight of human beings saying "Ya Basta! Enough is Enough!"[45]

I quote at length here to allow the performativity of Dominguez's text to play itself out. I want to focus on the operation of inventing an entire field of technology, in this case Mayan Technology. While this invention may seem imaginary or fictional, I claim that it is transreal, between fiction and non-fiction. Dominguez's assertion that his projects the Electronic Disturbance Theater (EDT) and *FloodNet*, a tool for creating virtual sit-ins that allow an audience of thousands to engage in mass nonviolent civil disobedience online, are Mayan

---

[45] "Ricardo Dominguez, Artist and Electronic Civil Disobedience Pioneer: Gothamist", accessed January 5, 2012, http://gothamist.com/2004/11/29/ricardo_dominguez_artist_and _electronic_civil_disobedience_pioneer.php.

Technology demonstrates an act of an artist prototyping an instance of a possible trajectory of technology and demonstrates the nonlinear causality at play in Mayan Technology. While FloodNet is an actual tool, functional code to enable mass participation in disturbing a target website, such as the website of the government of Mexico, the Minutemen or the University of California Office of the President, Dominguez still describes it as a lo-fi gesture that basically relies on simple html to programmatically press the reload button on the browser over and over. As such, FloodNet is a prototype for later tools that demonstrate much more sophistication and technical effectiveness, for example the Low Orbit Ion Cannon (LOIC) used by the group Anonymous to take offline the websites of the Church of Scientology, the Recording Industry Association of America, Visa and Mastercard.[46]

In addition, the effectiveness of FloodNet is not entirely clear, which can be seen as an example of Mayan Technology's reconsideration of simple linear causality. In some cases, the amount of disruption of the target web sites is minimal or not visible to website visitors, while in others, the target websites become totally inaccessible. In legal cases against Dominguez and collaborators, the point has been repeatedly raised that the

---

[46] "How Operation Payback Executes Its Attacks", accessed January 5, 2012, http://mashable.com/2010/12/09/how-operation-payback-executes-its-attacks/.

gesture is intended to be as performative and poetic as it is technically effective.

Yet a clearer nonlinear causality similar to Pedrito's stick often occurs when a virtual sit-in is simply announced. After announcing a virtual sit-in against the website of the government of France, in solidarity with French students on strike against the CPE,[47] the French equivalent of the U.S. Computer Emergency Response Team (CERT) contacted Calit2, The California Institute for Telecommunications and Information Technology, Dominguez's home institution at UCSD. They asked why the virtual sit-in was being planned and asked that the action be ended. This display of power by the French government demonstrates a kind of nonlinear, nonrational causality where the imagined fear of a virtual sit-in causes formerly hidden structures of power to reveal themselves. One of the strongest potentials that performance art has is to bring structures of power, which seem hidden and innocuous under contemporary regimes of biopolitics, to the stage, forcing them to reveal themselves and their violence. Dominguez's Mayan Technology performs a field of development that imagines its own transreal logic, separate from the science

---

[47] "Virtual Sit-In in Solidarity with the Striking Students of France! | post.thing.net", accessed January 5, 2012, http://post.thing.net/node/767.

resulting from Western rationalism whose logical outcome has produced digital technology.

While digital systems of computation rely on their ability to be compiled into binary code and Boolean logic, Reza Negarestani's book *Cyclonopedia* imagines a theoretico-fictional numogrammatical system based on the geometry of a specific relic, the Cross of Akht. The cross is said to have "the ability to numerically grasp all the undercurrents and inconsistent events of the Earth as modes of narration... through Oil."[48] Looking at the limits of the digital and technology writing that stays within the realm of the "real," the Cross of Akht demonstrates how transreal aesthetics can facilitate the creation of entirely new models of computation outside of the confines of the rational. While the current digital systems that many people interact with on a daily basis are ultimately reduced to computations represented by a 0 or a 1, Negarestani's book imagines a computational system that can represent nine numbers. The system derives from the artifact's ability to fold across nine different points. Throughout this work of metafiction, with stories contained within stories, Negarestani develops imaginary systems of thought to grapple with the massive conflicts across the Middle East, whose sheer reality in terms of numbers of civilians killed, for example, is seemingly incomprehensible.

---

[48] Reza Negarestani, Cyclonopedia: Complicity with Anonymous Materials (re.press, 2008), 13.

The Cross is at the root of many of these stories, and is described as having fantastical abilities of storytelling and diagramming, which I imagine are a metaphor for Negarestani's own multifaceted approach to folding realities together to produce a work of wild imagination. Negarestani says "the Cross of Akht, and its transformations, offer a diagram for the intrepid blasphemy of the Middle East against all modes of global hegemony and political models which perceive global dynamics as a whole."[49] While Negarestani's project intervenes at the level of hardware, imagining physical devices to build fantastical narrative systems on top of, other artists such as Zach Blas have imagined computational systems as software.

Zach Blas's project *Queer Technologies*[50] imagines trajectories for technology based on queer embodiments, times and spaces. The transCoder application programming interface (API) that Blas invented defines a series of function calls (named "sets of actions") that are not named based on common programming metaphors such as "string in C" or "moses in Puredata" but instead on metaphors from queer theory such as "fistingAsFriendship()" from the Foucault library and "qTime()"

------

[49] Reza Negarestani, *Cyclonopedia: Complicity with Anonymous Materials*, 14.
[50] "Queer Technologies", Zach Blas, accessed on January 9, 2012, http://www.queertechnologies.info.

from the Halberstam library.[51] In the mode of Critical Code Studies, one can explore the qualities of code itself to ask broader social questions, such as who is the audience for a particular programming language, what are that audience's assumptions and how do they limit the possible usages of code. Blas's transCoder opens up a wide chasm of possibilities by creating technologies that are not only functional for business purposes based on heteronormative assumptions. If programming languages are being used today for Web-based pansexual queer projects such as the NoFauxxx queer porn website or for queer performance art such as my own work with Elle Mehrmand, than having a language built with queer assumptions from the beginning can be seen as a logical step towards enabling creators like ourselves to write better software. TransCoder successfully reveals the limitations and assumptions of the culture of programming languages, as both students of technology and practitioners of computer science often balk and giggle at the mention of transCoder's functions. Yet for the queer media activist community and the sex hacking community,[52] having a library of functions that make up the

---

[51] "TransCoder | zach blas", accessed January 5, 2012, http://www.queertechnologies.info/products/transcoder/
[52] A very dedicated and rich community including such projects as Slashdong.org, PSIgasm.net and many others regularly seen at the Arse Elektronika conference every year in San Francisco, where I have had the good fortune of presenting my work on two occasions.

applications they are using can both make writing the code easier and reduce the amount of code that needs to be written to make functions written for other purposes do what is desired in these cases. Still, what is most interesting to me about transCoder is the possibility of imagining entire lines of technological development, such as queer technology, that can present other worlds and other logics, rooted in programming practices of today but imagining possibilities partly fictional, or transreal, in the present. TransCoder can be seen as a prototype of the concept of queer technologies, but still an imaginary prototype. Blas has developed other queer technology prototypes such as the Gay Bombs and the Facial Weaponization Suite, continuing to imagine applications for queer politics in technological devices.[53]

In my work with Elle Mehrmand, we have created a number of working prototypes of sexual technologies and imaginary computational systems with affective interfaces.

The chapter "Technésexual Interface" describes my performance in collaboration with Elle Mehrmand entitled *technésexual* (2009–2010). For the performance, we wore heartrate monitors and temperature sensors while we stripped and made out in front of a live audience. Simultaneously for an

---

[53] "Queer Technologies | zach blas", accessed January 5, 2012, http://www.zachblas.info/projects/queer-technologies-2/.

audience in Second Life, our avatars also kissed for the thirty-minute duration of the performance. The sound of our live heartbeats was played for both audiences in real time and at the actual rate our hearts were beating, and the pitch shifted according to our body temperatures, creating an organic interface for making music. "Technésexual Interface" proposes a model of interfaces that can be organic, responding to the state of internal organs of the body, allowing for a more intersubjective and cooperative model of computing.

The installation of *virus.circus.mem* (2011) presented at the "Speculative" exhibition at Los Angeles Contemporary Exhibitions imagines a speculative computational system that runs on ejaculate fluid. The installation includes displays of biometric data including heart rate graphs from the performances of *virus.circus.probe* and a wavelet coherence graph comparing the R-R intervals, or the space, in milliseconds, between each heartbeat of the performers during the performance. As the video plays, the viewer sees an inexplicable ritual unfolding as a glass dildo is used to interact with the biometric projections and the performers masturbate to orgasm on and above the table. As an experimental performance, the purposes, drives and desires in the piece are never explicitly spelled out, but in the context of the *virus.circus* series and it's meta texts, it can be inferred that the two characters are attempting to create their own Do-It-Yourself medicine as a form of resistance to the hegemonic fear narratives of viral infection with which they are constantly presented. The performances engage in prototyping by creating actual biometric sensing erotic electronic fashions, by mixing the physical with the virtual and through a nonlinear narrative that envisions resistance in a future where biopolitics is even more demanding of our physical bodies, forcing them to be contained in latex and masks at all times. *virus.circus.mem* explores how the erotic moments of two queer femmes can create an excess of breathing, looking and touching that can disturb the rational systems of Western medicine and biocapital, a femme disturbance. Through their excessive drive to explore their own biologies and bodies through femme clothing such as latex bras that are deconstructed by hand and resewn with conductive thread, the characters in *virus.circus.mem* resist the laws of Western medicine that restrict medical knowledge and practice to only a few experts. By engaging in such bodily risks and erotic explorations in public, the queer characters in *virus.circus.mem* challenge the heteronormative Western rationalism and its separation of public and private that seems to banish sex to the bedroom only to foreground heterosexual sex in advertising and media everywhere. The radical gesture though, is to encourage the exploration of and knowledge of the body with a goal of bodily autonomy, despite narratives of power that seek to determine a person's corporeal existence before one has had a chance to define the body oneself.

The erotic experiments in *virus.circus* follow an aesthetic trajectory of sex without skin-to-skin contact, responding to the transreal narrative based in part on real experiences of confluence of the military and medicine with H1N1 and actual queer and trans femme sexual practices and in part on imagined futures. Through a mixed reality gesture, *virus.circus.mem* also disturbs the audiences' ideas of contagion by presenting them with objects used for sex in the videos in the installation presented on the table in front of them, without letting them know whether these are in fact the same objects or if there is in fact any virus in question as the title suggests, or if this memory from the future has yet to happen. Ultimately, *virus.circus.mem* and the technologies it imagines seek to present audiences with acts and scenarios that are unfamiliar to them, reconfiguring their notions of intimacy to include detailed biometric readouts and pixilated avatar bodies, deterritorializing their ideas of sex to include scenes in which the amorous partners never touch or only touch each other with metal instruments, using reality as a medium, creating 3-dimensional displays, actual installations and embodied performances of unrecognizable futures.

The book you now hold in your hands is a creolized mixture of theory, poetry, fiction, source code, technical diagrams, photography and autobiography, a transreal gesture in itself consisting of speculations on futures, theorizations of performative gestures and an archive of past moments of transition between realities and genders. The introduction that I have laid out here should serve as a theoretical framework by describing the three major operations of the transreal: reality construction, transreal performativity and transreal technologies. I have attempted to show the broad relevance of the idea of creating multiple realities as demonstrated by numerous political actors and show the usage of these methods by other contemporary artists as well as in my own work and my collaborations with Elle Mehrmand. What follows are more details about each of our performances and analyses of those performances.

Becoming Transreal

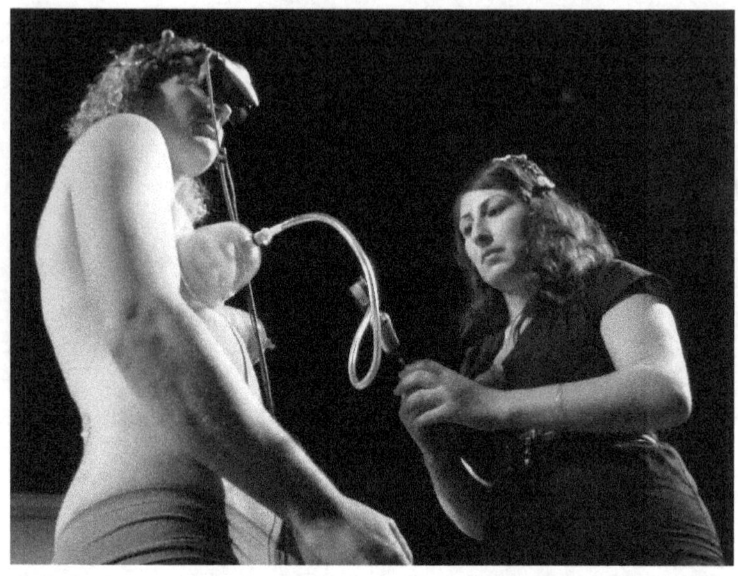

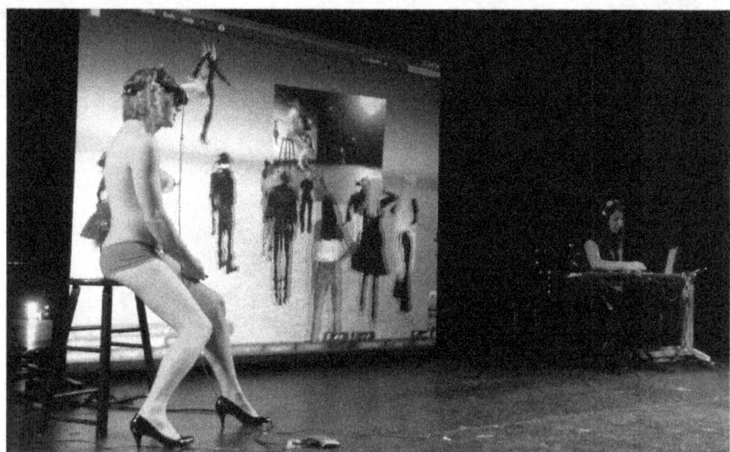

Becoming Transreal (2010), UCLA Freud Playhouse,

Photo: Tracy Cornish

Looking in the mirror I see a curve at the bottom of my breast for the first time. I'm ecstatic. Apparently the drug nanofactories in my blood are working, producing lots of progesterone, creating hypertrophy. Running into the living room asking Elle to take a photo– But she's reading and doesn't really want to be bothered. I say, "babe, I have boobs!" She says, "yeah, I know, I've been looking at them." She's not as astonished and excited as me, seeming to say they've always been there, but I think she's just being sweet. Photos in the mirror always look like shit, with the camera included and bad angles and faces and never close enough to approximate reality. It seems like something we're all supposed to be good at by now, sexy photos of ourselves for facebook. But after that creepy comment on flickr from that guy telling me to post more photos of my "development", I've reconsidered that drive to share my growth process with the world. For now I'm only selling my motion capture feed, holding back the streaming video for a bit.

A group of terrorists on Thursday were found in connection with a plot to infect themselves with VURTI's, threatening millions with acute viral rhinopharyngitis spread via the nanonet. The CDC taskforce for domestic health was able to identify them via their intermittent nanonet access and swiftly neutralized the threat. CDC officials say they have captured ten members of the a-coryza network in the city of Socal this month alone. The plots underscore a-coryza's interest in lower-level attacks that do not require the intricate planning and coordination of the Sept. 11, 2001, attacks. They also conform to a trend in which the terrorist network has used operatives already in potential target countries, rather than trying to sneak particles across increasingly secure borders.

Rolling around in bed with Elle, her on top of me, doing something amazing, looking at me sweetly, in the low red light from the curtains. I think "this is what is must be like for lesbians," and the thought surprises me. I think I'm becoming more comfortable slipping into that label, lesbian. For a while I thought of myself as pansexual, but somehow this makes the most sense now. Although one of the prescribed effects of prometrium is to change one's desire from the desire for women to desire for men, creating a "female desire", that is not happening to me. Lots of our closest friends are lesbians. Those are amazing moments, like yesterday, standing outside of a restaurant in Long Beach, windy, sun about to go down, just us girls, with nanofactories selling their wares in our bloodstreams. I try not to be too loud or overbearing and just be one of the crowd. Some people give me longer than normal glances, but laughing with our friends, I don't give a fuck.

We are interrupting the flows, rerouting, building our own networks of piracy, illicit trade in transformative nanopharmaceuticals. My body is a pharmacopoeia, both a drug factory and a book of instructions for drug production, nanomachines pumping and flashing in my organs. By sharing the trade secrets in my flesh, I can subvert the networks of digital and particle capital, undermine the war against autonomous forms. My participation in nanobiocapital creates hypertrophy, accelerating the growth and swelling of my breasts, but with these suction pumps, we can open up leaks, subvert the drug delivery, milk myself for the drugs my body is producing.

prometrium 100mg.

After our last performance, Felipe told Echolalia he liked her avatar because she wasn't recognizably anything, just sexual tension in every part of her body. We transform over and over again, experiment on top of experiment until our forms are unrecognizable assemblages of parts and characteristics, soft here, aggressive there, superfem there, bobby pins, medusa jellyfish tentacles, sweet tits and hard cock. (and perhaps skin a bit grey, spots faded, tired of so many changes) We don't have names for them any longer, just affective states. If as Amy Sara Carroll says, visceral realism is post-post modern, then this return to diving deep into the complexities and mysteries and pleasures of the flesh must be too. If reason itself is a western invention, part of colonialism, then is the future of thought to be poetry? Poetry of the flesh, intensive gradations of feeling and wordless thought, movements inside the body, states where planes of color bleed and shift into each other? Music, long hypnotic bass tones under high tenuous tones, the interplay of muscles and intramuscular senses like stretch receptors, not the truth of visual observation, or of 5 senses, but an ongoing experience of a rich network of proprioceptive senses.

I wake up and my tits hurt. It's morning. It's like they've been pushing and stretching and yearning to get out of my chest all night. It's such a satisfying soreness.

Distrito Federal. The sprawling megalopolis of all our futures. We fly in over black glass buildings, all antennas and red lights. Sheer complexity, the networks of lights sprawling out as far as the eye can see, in different patterns, amber fields of veins, sparkling lights like the hills of Tijuana. On our way to Chiapas, our layover is in D.F. I think I was about fifteen when I decided to make my life into art, as a way to process, to deal with my mother's schizophrenia. Today its assumed that our every moment, every gesture, everything we see, is immediately sent into the network. As an erotic electronic artist that is further compounded, our most intimate moments make up the content of our work and our free time is indecipherable from work. We are the product and the factory, our bodies, our cells, our lives, our thoughts and imaginations.

Wittig's lesbian body is blood and pain and dirt. Kathy Acker's queer body is "fiery storms and other catastrophic phenomena." Mine is more soreness, longing and the inexplicable. Sore tits, longing to have another body and the mind that goes with it, and the unexplainable way I act sometimes, like when my hormone levels are off from missing a production delivery out to the nanonet or being on the last day of my patch. Žižek says liberation hurts, but this is a whole different kind of revolution outside of his dialectic. Now, even my cock hurts. My doctor doesn't know why either, says it's not expected but nothing serious. When I get up to piss at night, my urethra hurts. It may be all the tight clothes, since my body is growing most of my clothes are too tight now, but my doctor says it may be the output from chemical changes in my body.

Elle gets stopped at security. In her purse, the RFID tracker from the hacker gathering we just left is still on, blinking red with exposed circuitry, capacitors and lead tracings, the words "The Next HOPE" etched into the board. Security is puzzled. She asks me to translate. I struggle to explain "es un objeto estética, una cosa de belleza". My Spanish should be better, but after the divorce my mom didn't want us to speak Spanish in the house because it reminded her of dad, which made her more depressed. He tells us "Esta bien, pase" and we're through. Three days of so-called mobility is exhausting. My ass is killing me. On the customs form, along with my nationality and my date of birth I have to specify my gender. This is increasingly worrysome as I wonder if the migración officers will stop me because of the mismatch of the M in my passport and my appearance. But it's just wishful thinking, that they might notice my boobs. Out of context, in sweats and a t-shirt they're probably invisible. Even though I got my new passport with a new picture I like with my longer hair and decent eye makeup, I didn't get the M changed to an F, or anything else. That's legal now, but the law changed right after I got mine. We land in Chiapas, everything green and wet.

Catorce dias en chiapas, estudiando con la Fortaleza de Mujer Maya. Am I passing better here because some people think all americans are too tall? Or are people just more polite than in New York? Or do they just want a good tip? The warm, sweet grandmother who seems to own the hotel we're staying in sits with her family and every time we come and go they stare at us through the windows. Is it because we're American or because I'm a tranny? Did I put on too much eyeliner this morning? Sitting, listening to a talk on indigenous women's oppression, I am struck by a wave of dizzyness and nausea. I feel like an alien here under attack from a jungle of foreign bacteria.

I know the risks, that domestic biosecurity forces in masks may show up at the doorsteps of pirates and those who would create their own autonomous networks of information, but to struggle for a world where people can change their bodies freely, the risk is worth it. We have to find ways to move freely while being motion captured, to imagine bodily insurrection through monstrous forms while swimming in images of perfect statuesque bodies with ideal features magnified to grotesque proportions. Everywhere around me is the image of the perfect body, but I want to exploit the medical system to give me an assortment of parts that is unimaginable and unnamable. I decided along the way that I want to have this body and this life outside of the names I used to have for myself, and now I have it.

Back home to the borderlands, today was my first time wearing a bikini in public, or, well, not counting performances, ok, my first time swimming in a bikini, and actually it was just my black bra and panties. "The dragon has arrived" D-boy said when we pulled up to the house. We hung out with the same friends we saw last 4th of July. All day we enjoyed their pool, everyone drinking and smoking out and eating brownies (If you don't smoke it, maybe you'll eat it, they said) All day LD stayed in the water, getting drunk and talking ridiculously. It was an amazing day to enjoy playing pool games, just one of the girls. Shana showed up last, with her boyfriend. It was pretty awkward, all the lesbians playing silly games in the pool and Shana walks in with her huge heels and her big pit/boxer and her boyfriend with the perfect mohawk and shiny tall combat boots. I think she felt ostracized from that moment on. It was my first time being on the inside of an insular lesbian social circle instead of the outside. I'm still not sure if that brownie had any effect. And Elle and I can't figure out either if D-boy is actually a sub slave or not. We had amazing vegan tacos with organic olive oil from the co-op just before everyone passed out and Elle and I drove home, since we live close. Before we leave, I have a rare moment with myself in the bathroom mirror, getting back into comfy clothes, where I feel like I really look good.

It is well known that the police kick down doors and raid homes to protect intellectual property, and yet the networks of piracy go even farther. As more and more secrets are released of the pharmacopoeia and about the perpetual wars, the questions increasingly shift to necropolitics and the question of not only how to do what we want with our bodies, but how to keep more bodies alive.

Before our morning stimulants we can be vicious. Crying behind my sunglasses. Looking for a private spot in the shade on campus, I settle on the motion capture lab as the place to put my head on the desk and cry. Ronell, "the age of the chemical prosthesis has already begun."

What we try not to think about is that the medical industry
making a profit in our blood, and not just with the medical-
military complex. The medical system failed my mom.
Diagnosed with schizophrenia 20 years ago, the illnesses pile on:
diabetes, cancer, and now maybe dementia from chemotherapy?
All the while, they're making money off of her. The year I
gained a breast, she lost one. The nanobio industry has failed
her, and "rational pharmacology" is still a horizon. I usually cry
after I talk to her, yesterday she told me she thought her doctor
visit was in Chatanooga, Tennessee, when its really in Miami.
She's thinking of her brother, but can't distinguish the memory
from reality. I refuse to accept what my sister says, that the mom
we know "isn't there any more," because I love her too much to
accept it.

I am finding my voice. I've finally decided to change my voice. While Echolalia was traveling with her family, I spent two weeks practicing my new voice everyday. The drugs I download everyday are successfully fabricating 3-dimensional biocompatible nanoparticle assemblies so well, that I've begun to get a taste of passing with my new body. I think that taste has me wanting more, or being more frustrated with the disjuncture between my voice and my appearance. I turn on the videostreams from other shapeshifters and learn from them how to do weight lifting with my throat. Half of the population is taught, very subtly, almost imperceptibly, to keep their throat muscles high and constricted when they speak, or are we just taught to think it's not happening. The other half is taught to leave their larynx relaxed. I have simply decided to retrain myself and create a new voice.

We are becoming transreal. Our identities span realities. Now that the possibility exists for any bodily transformation, to become any gender one wants with enough time and money and willingness to bleed, we want more. We want to be real and unreal at the same time, to span realities, to be multiple, a digital body and a physical body, and also multiple digital bodies, alts, bots, clones. Are you talking to one of my bots, or clones, or to me? Does it make a difference? Is sex with a clone infidelity? I am fleeing regimes of identification and visibility. I reject anyone's ability to ask me if I'm a real woman, because real woman is a fantasy. Our lives are a rapid series of switches between registers, swapping out levels of real sensor(y) experience, fantasy, symbolic names we have for ourselves. And, as Ronell says, existing on multiple registers simultaneously.

I feel relieved that I will have to get one less surgery, now that I have the muscle memory in place to use my vagus nerve how I desire, emanating more identifiably female intonations. Still, again, as I've gained this, my mother is losing her ability to speak. Every conversation I have with her informs me of her worsening condition. The doctors aren't helping. Her dementia worsens, she makes no sense, and at times, she mumbles unintelligible sounds. Her voice doesn't sound like her own. Some moments, she sounds like someone else. My sister tells me that we should be patient, keep calling, trying to bring her a little joy, that it helps. She tells me that mom is just communicating in a different way and we should learn to talk to her. More learning to talk and learning to listen. Mom's slipping into another reality, becoming transreal, like me. But aren't we all?

193~181~250~160~189~150~210~ The question of passing becomes a question of the ability to maintain an oscillation above 175 hertz, around 220, now that the factories in my DNA have synthesized inorganic-polypeptide systems into 2- and 3-dimensional arrays enough for my breasts and tentacles to show. When Elle told her mother I was on hormones, her response was "*yeah*, I saw her boobs!" For my voice, I talk to the computer to see the teal blue spectrogram scrolling, it's invaluable for the process. After training with a frequency analyzer, I feel like I can speak again. In the store, ordering coffee, in a restaurant ordering food, to co-workers, all my exchanges with people are transformed. Where once I had been prevented from trying on clothes at a Target, told to use the men's changing room, now I try on my new bra without a second glance. The struggle is to maintain the training when talking to my lover, when it is unncessary. She is so gracious in seeing her lover change before her eyes, a new voice warm in her ear. Still, I have a newfound form of feminine expression. A sheer joy in talking, out loud, to myself, alone, feeling like someone new.

"Can you see me behind my sunglasses?"

"Yeah, can you see me?"

"Yes."

Lying naked on the beach, looking into each other's eyes. After the police have come and gone and the investigations of our copyright violations, illicit communications, leaks and GPS signals, are over, the soft weapon of bureaucracy lifting itself from our lives, for now, for a moment, we take a break from figuring out our futures and play in the freezing cold waves, rubbing our hard nipples together, kissing, laughing, screaming, getting knocked down by one huge wave and laughing more. The rays of sun on the silver gray ocean are beautiful, but this moment between us, looking at each other and sharing so much love and lust, is something else, something wordless.

Becoming Transreal Panel

Ricardo Dominguez

I'll just touch on a few things in terms of the history of thought that the Critical Art Ensemble and Electronic Disturbance Theater have imagined in a very rudimentary form in the '80s and '90s. The performative matrix would bring together data bodies and real bodies in a space of encounter that would consolidate these bodies or mix them up in order to disturb the oncoming rush of different virtual capitalism(s) that would emerge in the '90s.

This performative matrix of data bodies and real bodies was imagined as a counter to the future bodies that were given over to a kind of pure machinic stage and instead were imagined as bodies that added another level of disturbance to those conditions of a pure machinic body. A third or forth body, another type of prosthetic emerging out of the data body and real body encountering itself would be the product of three poles or intensities between the data body and the real body - in the '90s we imagined it as being a configuration between bodies with organs, bodies without organs and organs without bodies. In a certain sense the structure of *Becoming Transreal* allows these different shapes, in a new gesture, to appear. It wasn't exactly the way that we imagined the data body and real body to interconnect.

Certainly the issue of Second Life performance or performativities allows us both to subtract from that original idea of the performative matrix and at the same time to look at new amplifications of it. The question about what is subtracted from the original idea of the performative matrix was that the merger of data bodies and real bodies would manifest itself as an element that would be in contestation to the conditions of virtual capitalism(s).

One of the questions that I have for the performers and the performance is to what degree does Second Life consolidate this kind of socioeconomic base of technology, rather than disturb it, so that it becomes a lure of a type of techno-capital avatarism, or on the utopian end of the performative matrix of *Becoming Transreal* is the possibility of surprising new organs, surprising organs that are unexpected both to the rushing capitalism(s) that are transforming the sense of space around us both in first life and Second Life so that *Becoming Transreal* is also diagramming surprising new organs that are no longer strictly bound to a body without organs, or to a body with organs or organs without a body - but indeed a new condition that is being engineered by the trans-individuals processing it. That is to seek out in *Becoming Transreal* a surprising trans-organ, surprising trans-organism, of what is the most anti-anti-utopian edge of the performative matrix at this moment of becoming trans-real.

Allucquére Rosanne Stone

As these performances become more sophisticated over the years, we reach a point at which the discourse itself becomes more real. It takes on a life of its own that is partially grounded in the performance, but I think this is a very good thing, going beyond it. The topic of how an imagined body or a techno body, a digital body is placed in space and time in those circumstances becomes very rich. I've been watching these performances of various kinds, not just the ones that are going on here but others as well all over the world for close to twenty years now.

What I see happening with the work that Azdel (micha) is doing is to carry things beyond the simple impressions of space and time that we play with here within multiple planes of what is actually a 2D environment but which works like an environment beyond three dimensions. Incorporating other axes and other tensors into that equation so that you produce by virtue of your movements and by virtue of the medium that we're working in a dimension of emotion, a dimension of reaching out, a dimension of voice, each one of which can open up in different respects.

The bringing together the body without organs, the organic body and the things for which we don't have any words here in the area of the transreal makes room for different kinds of consciousnesses. We see that here even in the way that the people who are visiting this performance look. This kind of look wouldn't have been possible a while ago. The increase in bandwidth, the increase in speed of the processor chips and the increase of the sophistication and knowledge and the delicacy of approach of the people who are engaged in these performances as I'm watching them have already taken us into a different form of viewing, participating and ways in which our concept of our own bodies have transcended what we could do before.

I want to just touch on a coupe of points, some of which are old. One of them is the three-C approach to this, that is that Code Creates Community. The bases of this kind of world and the interactions that it facilitates are based in a very specific digital origin and manipulation. It's a code, but it's not the kind of social code that I might be talking about here, it's the actual making of the world through acts of will, through imperative gestures which are specifically digital in nature and which lead to beyond three, multi-dimensional worlds that we're dealing with here, including organic and inorganic dimensions that we're just beginning to see.

Amy Sara Carroll

In a sense, my situation is the opposite of Sandy's. This is only my second day in Second Life, so everything is new and wondrous for me, a still too shiny learning experience. And, from the standpoint of such beginnings, I am struck by the sheer potentials that Second Life offers for poetry readings and for performance. I love the ways in which we can travel through presence and absence, fall down, and emerge from, rabbit and wormholes, come and go, become interpellated and help to interpellate others, seen and unseen, into new configurations of participant-observation—speculative futures of and for a material and performative poetics—here.

For instance, (the figures or characters of) Azdel and Echolalia anticipate, manipulate, and fold into their presentation today so-called technical glitches. Namely, the name "Echolalia"— a word derived from the Greek that means to echo or repeat—might be understood to reference the function of the figure "Echolalia" in *Becoming Transreal*, her repetition with a difference of Azdel's poems. But, her name also could reference the medium's propensity to multiply the echo, to render "Echolalia" herself transreal. For, if Echolalia echoes Azdel; the technologies (of gender) of SL allow Echolalia to come into her own polyvocally, to come out, to be echoed *ad infinitum*.

Or, concretely speaking, at first I could not get the sound to work on my computer in SL ("the queer art of failure"). Then, with the help of new and old friends, the kindness of strangers, suddenly sound was everywhere for me. Second Life, like Echolalia, echoed text in real time as surely as it elongated silences. Now as I listen and virtually move through SL, a part of this performance, all noise—from white to pink, across an even wider spectrum of the every day—wave-like becomes the omnipresence of a second, third, fourth…"Echolalia," other cyborg-goddess-tricksters in the machine that expand the frame of the conversation. (And, when I send a message to the community to ask how I can remedy this situation, my interlocutors respond that it's par for the course.)

In turn, this special effect, surely a continuum of special affects, corresponds to, but amplifies, the loops already inscribed in the poems themselves. On the page, what Azdel has read/performed comes together as a luminous collection of twenty-one prose poems (with that number, this critic cannot help but recall Adrienne Rich's "Twenty-One Love Poems"). Indebted to confessional poetry, to speculative and science fictions, to 1970s feminism/s, to third wave feminism/s, to queered and racialized critical theories, to the cultures of social media and networks, "Becoming Transreal" contemplates the gaining and losing of voice as such processes intersect with further adventures in identity, identification, and spatiotemporal transformation ("I am finding my voice. I've finally decided to change my voice" [75]; "The question of passing becomes a question of the ability to maintain an oscillation above 175 hertz, around 220.... I have a new found form of feminine expression. A sheer joy in talking, out loud, to myself, alone feeling like someone new" [78]).

A "Telephone Book": Hello Wittig. Hello Acker. Hello Žižek. Hello Ronell, "[T]he age of the chemical prosthesis has already begun" (73). I repeat, "We transform over and over again, experiment on top of experiment until our forms are unrecognizable assemblages of parts and characteristics soft here, aggressive there, superfem there, bobby pins, medusa jellyfish tentacles, sweet tits and hard cock" (even myself quoted, blinking back at me (the "Amy Sara Carroll")—"Did I say that?"—some textual tchotchke in an Arcades Project!) (64).

"Becoming Transreal" marks and unmarks relationships among voice, voices, and the nebulous expanding categorization of the transreal. Resisting an aesthetics, a politics of the real, "Becoming Transreal" punctuates the critical difference the prefix "trans-," itself about movement or passage, enables. Not (only) about clarity or concretude, "trans-" gender- and genre-troubles the reader's or spectator's buried desires for documentation, location, identification, development, growth. "I look in the mirror" is quickly juxtaposed with the fantastical, albeit ominous, reference to "the drug nanofactories in my blood" (59). The ultrabaroque scenario of "A group of terrorists on Thursday were found in connection with a plot to infect themselves with VURTI's" (60) comes up against the minimalist simplicity of "prometrium 100 mg." The admission, "I think I'm

becoming more comfortable slipping into that label, lesbian"
(61), is rerouted with and by the observation, "Shana showed up
last, with her boyfriend. It was pretty awkward…" (61).

So many ways, waves, and forms to police and be policed
by! Yet, a "rolling around in bed" remains; "[w]e want to be real
and unreal at the same time" (76). Hot flashes of self/other
recognition endow this poetry with its extrasensory perceptions,
its abilities to induce, anticipate, and honor any number of
unexpected instantiations of echolalia. In this spirit, it seems
important to recall that the medical establishment classifies
"echolalia" as a symptom of, or as present in autism, in other so-
called "developmental disorders," including Tourette syndrome,
in schizophrenia, and in Alzheimer's disease.

And, buried in narratives that are as much about
constancy and certitude as they are about transformation and
flux, is empathic hospitality, a recognition of the parallel tracks
of change vis-à-vis the figure of the maternal, the mother: "She's
slipping into another reality, becoming transreal, like me. But
aren't we all?" (77) (or, earlier, a bald intimacy doubles as
artistic genealogy: "I think I was about 15 when I decided to
make my life into art, as a way to process, to deal with my
mother's schizophrenia" [66]; or, an ironic accusation that
follows the money, "The medical system failed my mom…. The
year I gained a breast, she lost one" [74]).

Aren't we all? The challenge of this performance, one echo
of this collection, is that of apprehending (hearing, seeing,

tasting, "touching feeling") its unique echoes (or not) in ourselves, "a rich network of proprioceptive senses" (64). "'Can you see me behind my sunglasses?'" (79). Can we rise to the occasion of not only simulating, but inhabiting, the subject position/s of "Echolalia"—her silences, synapses, lapses—as "Becoming Transreal"'s readers and observers? Jacques Derrida famously situated texts, total speech situations, as echo-chambers, foregrounding their side effects, his différance, to be that of echolalia. Second Life renders literal Derrida's conceit in Azdel's and Echolalia's performance of *Becoming Transreal*, in this panel's discussion of the performance.

> Becoming transreal?
>
> "… this moment between us, looking at each other and sharing so much love and lust, is something else, something wordless" (79).
>
> *Todos somos Echolalia.*

Technésexual Interface
Erotic Mixed Reality Performance

Micha Cárdenas and Elle Mehrmand

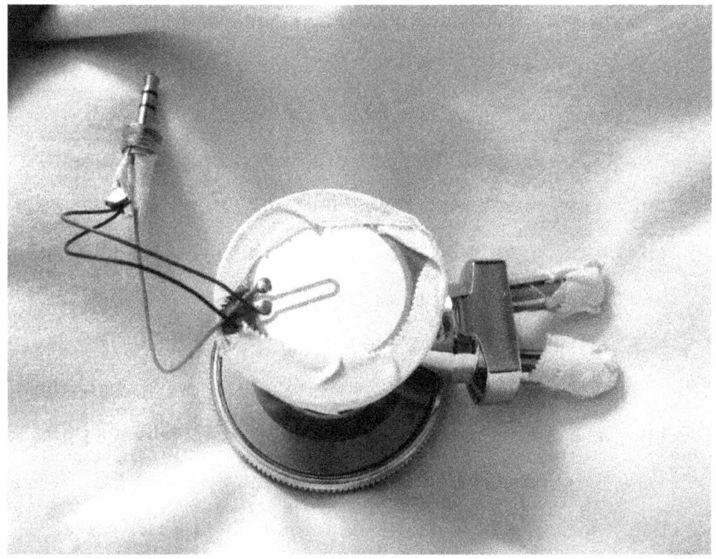

technésexual (2009), Hemispheric Institute of Performance and Politics VII Encuentro, Bogotá, Colombia. Photo: Micha Cárdenas and Elle Mehrmand

Biometric sensors, made cheaply available by do-it-yourself (DIY) prototyping platforms such as Arduino, allow a shift away from visual interfaces to proprioceptive interfaces, away from the touch of a finger and towards a more internal, embodied form of sensing. One possible effect of this shift is away from the command-control methodology, which was a historical basis for cybernetics, and towards a form of modulation and cooperation akin to intersubjectivity. In this chapter, we will consider recent writings on interface relevant to the shift from external to internal, or from haptic to organic, discuss our experiences creating and using them, and explore some of the implications of this shift.

As an illustrative example, we will discuss our work *technésexual*, a performance where we commit erotic acts in physical and virtual space simultaneously, using heart rate and temperature sensors to amplify and modulate the sound of our heartbeats for two audiences. This performance explores how relations between people, and between people and technology, change in Mixed Reality environments. *technésexual* uses the body as a musical instrument to produce sound with the Pure Data (Pd) programming language, in order to bridge the physical performance space and the 3-dimensional multi-user virtual environment of Second Life. The sounds of our heartbeats are also sent into Second Life and emanate from our avatars as they too commit erotic acts. This performance involves what we call an "organic interface," or a physical interface that responds to one's organs. Erotic touch becomes a way to activate the body and change its internal state.

Considering Interfaciality

Much recent writing about interface is concerned with the shifts in interface design enabled by new technologies. In her book *Materializing New Media*, Anna Munster writes that the focus on the face, representing instrumental rationality, has reinforced the mind/body split, and that this currently shapes much of interface design. She argues that there is a need for new media artists to expand interface design to incorporate much more of the human body, in order to allow for greater expressivity but also greater potential for transformative experience. Munster uses examples such as David Rokeby's *Very Nervous System*, an audio interface controlled by movement, and Char Davies's *Osmose*, a virtual reality interface controlled by breath.[54] She highlights the move towards an invisible interface, where the interface becomes an undefined space for experience. Munster states, "we need to radically rethink the interface in our modes of realizing our relations with the machine as the point of both contact surface and disappearance of the space of difference between humans and computers."[55] The organic interface in *technésexual* demonstrates this "disappearance" by internalizing the interface.

One of our main motivations with *technésexual* was to move beyond the focus on the visual in mixed and augmented reality applications. Alexander Galloway's recent essay "The Unworkable Interface" considers the trend towards the invisibility of interfaces. Galloway's writing has explored the shift from a disciplinary society as described by Michel Foucault to a control society as described by Gilles Deleuze. The move to a control society is precisely the internalization and embodiment

---

[54] Anna Munster, *Materializing New Media: Embodiment in Information Aesthetics*, annotated edition. (Dartmouth, 2006), 111.
[55] Ibid.

of power. Galloway writes that "windows, doors, airport gates, and other thresholds," examples of types of interfaces, controlling access to spaces, "are those transparent devices that achieve more the less they do: for every moment of virtuosic immersion and connectivity . . . the threshold becomes one notch more invisible."[56]

Discussing the example of World of Warcraft's complex interface, he proposes that to imagine an interface as something transparent is to oversimplify it and to ignore that there is an internal aspect of the interface itself, an internal relation, an "intraface." Galloway's analysis is important to our own thinking of organic interfaces in that our goal is not to create a totally transparent way of interacting with virtual worlds, but instead to open up new potentials for understanding and experiencing the body. Instead of abandoning the tradition of performance art using the body as a medium by moving towards virtual bodies, we seek to expand that tradition by finding rich interfaces in between the physical and virtual bodies. The notion of intraface underscores the power relations implicit in the form of an interface, implying that more liberatory structures can be imagined.

Important for a consideration of the transreal is that Galloway calls the intraface a "zone of indecision" citing Gérard Genette and says it is "*indecisive* for it must always juggle two

---

[56] Alexander R. Galloway, "The Unworkable Interface," *New Literary History* 39, no. 4 (2008): 931.

things (the edge and the center) at the same time."[57] The multiplicity of the intraface reflects the multiple realities of the transreal as well as it's ability to challenge simple conceptions of decision making based on the logical assumption of a single reality. Further, Galloway uses a performance example that has also helped the development of the concept of the transreal, the work of Augusto Boal. Moving from embodied experience to aesthetics to politics, Galloway says that

> Boal addresses himself to breaking down existing conventions within the expressive mode in order that mankind's political instinct might awaken. The edge of the work is thus an arrow pointing to the outside, that is, pointing to the actually existing social and historical reality in which the work sits. Genette's "indecision" is, in this light, a codeword for something else: *historical materialism.* The edges of the work are the politics of the work.[58]

In this discussion of interface, Galloway makes links between aesthetics and politics that resonate deeply with the concept of the transreal, as the interactions of the edges, where multiple realities collide, are precisely where transreal aesthetics can reveal political possibilities to viewers and participants.

The visual component of virtual experiences has been overdeveloped to the detriment of our many other senses, both exteroceptive, interoceptive and proprioceptive. If we consider

---

[57] "The Unworkable Interface", 944.
[58] Ibid., 945.

the many dimensions of our awareness of the internal state of our bodies, including not only balance and muscle positioning, but also stretch receptors in our muscles, we can begin to open a vast new possibility for interface design.

Previous Experiments with Physical Interfaces

Initially, the idea to use heart rate monitors came from a public conversation between Stelarc and Cárdenas in which Stelarc stated that "avatars have no organs."[59] We found this statement to be problematic, implying a clean separation between the physical body and the avatar body. In a way, our initial idea for *technésexual* was to create "avatars with organs."

Our interest in using DIY electronics emerged out of our previous work using different technologies to map positionality, including a Nintendo Wii and motion capture. In Mehrmand's *sextrument*, a live durational performance in which she masturbated for one hour, with a Nintendo Wii remote controller, she explored this notion of embodied interface. The accelerometer sensor in the Wii-mote measured the speed and intensity of her hand movement, which sent messages to MaxMSP, altering the sound of her voice. Behind a door, she invited viewers to look through a peephole, evoking anxiety and

---

[59] "Becoming Dragon, 3 Minute Documentation," micha cardenas, accessed on January 5, 2012, http://vimeo.com/3874238.

states of desire. She found the Wii-mote interface problematic as it was cumbersome.

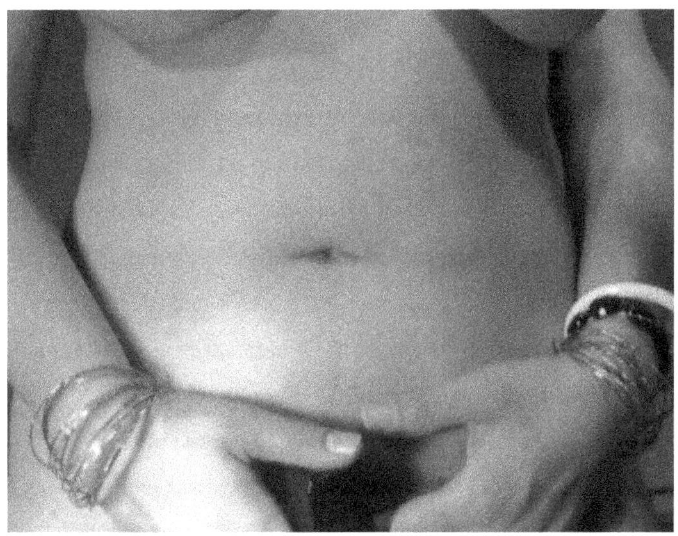

sextrument. (2008), performance/video. Photo: Elle Mehrmand

In *Becoming Dragon*, Cárdenas lived for 365 hours continuously in Second Life wearing a head-mounted display and markers that were tracked by a Vicon motion capture system, mapping her movements onto a dragon avatar in Second Life. The Vicon system was a frequent source of frustration, as the software was proprietary and unreliable. Motion capture also predisposed viewers to expect a literal one-to-one relation between her body and her avatar's, which felt limiting. From these experiences, we decided to focus on using cheaply accessible electronics components, combining shared interests in performance, the body, and desire.

Creating Organic Interfaces: Embodied Experimentation and Surprise

In its first analog rendition, *technésexual* was performed at the Hemispheric Institute for Performance and Politics in Bogotá, Colombia. Even this low-tech version of the performance introduced us to a new level of intimacy with each other and a new knowledge about each other's bodies. We attached a piezo sensor, acting as a contact microphone, to a stethoscope. Experimenting with the piezo, we could hear each other's heartbeats for the first time. We realized that many people might go through their lives without hearing the sound of their heartbeat, or their lover's heartbeat, that this was knowledge that had been kept to doctors.

Subsequent performances relied on a Polar heart rate monitor using an electrocardiogram, which worked through wet contact of the skin near the heart. The sensor detects the electrical pulse that creates a heartbeat and sends this data wirelessly to a polar receiver module. We soldered a bridge circuit so that this module could communicate with our Freeduino and Arduino using the I2C interface. The Arduino code, in a language based on C, must initiate communication and periodically request an array of data. One element of this array is a number representing the current beats per minute. The next component of our heart monitor interface is a USB connection to our computers. Our Arduino code sends the current heart rate over the USB serial ports of our computers, and a patch in the Pd graphical programming language listens to the serial port. This is accomplished using the comport object in Puredata-extended, and sending the heart rate to a sampler loop which plays a recording of each of our heartbeats at the current rate. Finally, the sound output from Pd is routed through a Presonus Firebox into the microphone input of Second Life using voice chat from each of our avatars, allowing the audio to be spatially located in Second Life as emanating from our avatars and causing the voice intensity indicator above their heads to pulse with a green glow.

A recent performance of *technésexual* at the Nevada Museum of Art included a temperature-based touch sensor. Using a thermistor, a resistor whose resistance varies in response to temperature, we are able to detect when one performer touches the other's body. This data is used to modulate the pitch of the heart rate up, controlling the sound by means of sensual touch. In this way our bodies become instruments, comparable to the way bagpipes have a drone, a continuous sound of air passing through the reeds, while having a chanter which can control the pitch (usually set two octaves higher than the drone) to play a melody.[60] In *technésexual* one can hear our heart rates at the actual rate continuously (the drone), in addition to hearing that same sample modulated at a higher pitch using the

---

[60] Anthony Baines, *Bagpipes* (Pitt Rivers Museum, 1979).

temperature sensors (the chanter) creating a new kind of interface for music making. The drone of the bagpipes is heard as long as the musician is pumping the bellows, the same way that our heartbeats are played as long as we are plugged in.

Our initial expectations were challenged through experimentation with the devices. We found that our heart rates when performing were considerably higher than at rest, and surprisingly, when we began kissing, our heart rates went down. At first, we wrote the Pd patch to work correctly with our resting heart rates observed in our studios, 65–70 for Cárdenas and 75–80 for Mehrmand. Yet when we did our performance with the devices at the annual GLAMFA exhibit, we found that our starting heart rates were between 105 and 115, causing noticeable audio glitches. After this we rewrote the patch to accommodate the higher heart rate by scaling the length of the playback to fit the current rate. Still, as the duration of the piece unfolds, between 15 and 30 minutes in different performances, we have discovered minute changes in our heart rates, up or down at particular moments, such as during touches to our body parts or the removal of particular pieces of clothing. We end the performance naked, and the amplification of our internal organs' states adds more depth to our degree of exposure, exposing what cannot be seen.

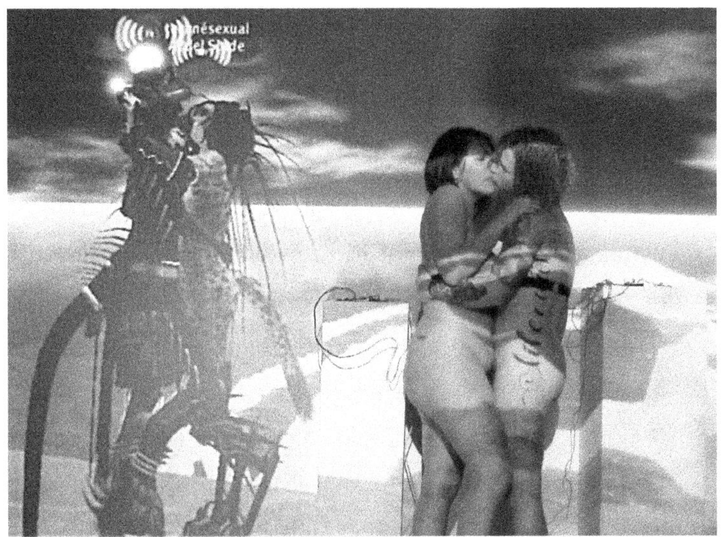

technésexual (2010), Los Angeles Contemporary Exhibitions,
GUTTED Annual Winter Benefit. Photo: Zach Blas and Marcela Coto

Erotic Touch

By performing *technésexual*, we found that organic interfaces
can add intimacy to a performance, and not just increased
intimacy, but different forms of it. We wanted to continue our
practices of durational performance art and relational
performance, engaging the dynamics of our own intimate
relationship. Inspired by the work of such artists as Marina
Abramovic and Ulay, Shu Lea Cheang and Lygia Clark, we
created instruments that allowed us to both be in mixed reality
simultaneously and create sound with the interaction of our
bodies. Using erotic touch, kissing, we activated our organs
directly, using our skin itself as a touch-based interface.

Through this process, we gained a different kind of understanding of our own intimate states, that of a deep comfort and relaxation, beyond our original conception of excitement. The audience is also invited to a deeper form of intimacy, with entirely new strata of connection between the viewer and the performer, as the interior of the performers' bodies becomes part of the audience's multisensory experience.

Audience members have described the performance to us as intense, as putting them in a trance and as making them sweat. We could also think of this work as creating erotic interfaces, as their use requires an intimate knowledge of one's body, close attention to the state of the body and an increased intimacy among the performers, the technology and the audience.

Through organic interfaces, we are opening up the liminal space of performance, making the performers' and the audiences' bodies porous and intermingled, encouraging an escape from subject-object, performer-audience and controller-controlled relationships.

Intersubjective Somatic Architecture

Another example of internalized interfaces has been proposed by Ricardo Dominguez, who writes that capitalism is shifting from multinational capitalism towards "particle capitalism or nano driven-technology."[61] He proposes that this shift is accompanied

------

[61] Ricardo Dominguez, "Particles of Interest: Tales from the

by a move from interface towards introjection, or the introjection of the interface. In this new condition the somatic architecture becomes part of the system of production. Dominguez is part of a collaboration called the Particle Group investigating this shift. On the Particle Group website, Dominguez writes, "her left breast was now selling almost all paclitaxel* 10 particles as the matter market cycle hit a high value exchange. 'How small can anything be?' . . . Her left breast was fading with each of the trespasses of her trans_patents—the cancer had been metastatic till now."[62] Such imaginings imply a possible future for organic interfaces in which people's organs are the site of production, and nanofactories in our own bodies enact a will other than our own, troubling notions of bodily autonomy. Perhaps organic interfaces made by artists can foster critical thinking about their implications and allow their future to be shaped differently.

Another possibility for interfaces, outside of encouraging control, is the possibility of intersubjective interfaces, as theorists such as Sherry Turkle have discussed.[63] One of our

---

Matter Market » Trans_patent: 5, 439,686", n.d., http://bang.calit2.net/pitmm/?p=33.

[62] Ibid.

[63] D. Fox Harrell, "Toward a Theory of Phantasmal Media: An Imaginative Cognition- and Computation-Based Approach to Digital Media", *CTheory* (2009), accessed on January 2, 2010, http://www.ctheory.net/articles.aspx?id=610#_ednref32.

main inspirations for thinking about the value of intersubjective
interfaces is Donna Haraway, who writes, "the partners do not
precede their relating: all that is, is the fruit of becoming with."[64]
The concept of "becoming with" resonates with our interest in
exploring our intersubjective experience of our intimate
relationship using mixed reality technologies.

As we consider the future of interfaces and nano-bots which
inhabit and commingle with our bodies, we can learn much from
the kind of feminist values Haraway employs: cooperation,
accountability and care. Haraway argues that "touch ramifies
and shapes accountability. . . Touch, regard, looking back and
becoming with—all these make us responsible in unpredictable
ways for which worlds take shape."[65] Still, this touch needs to be
considered in all of its complexity, reframing the earlier
disappearance of difference of Munster and the outside within
the inside of Galloway into an intersubjective commingling
without clear distinctions or identities. Haraway does this when
she considers interface and world-making, which can be seen as
very related to reality-building in the transreal:

> Technologies are organs, full partners, in what
> Merleau-Ponty called "infoldings of the flesh." I like
> the word *infolding* better than *interface* to suggest the

---

[64] Donna J. Haraway, *When Species Meet* (Univ Of Minnesota
Press, 2007), 36.
[65] Ibid.

dance of world-making encounters... Infoldings of the flesh *are* worldly embodiment. The word makes me see the highly magnified surfaces of cells shown by scanning electron microscopes. In those pictures, we experience in optic-haptic touch the high mountains and valleys, entwined organelles and visiting bacteria, and multiform interdigitations of surfaces we can never again imagine as smooth interfaces.[66]

With *technésexual*, we have attempted to find a line of flight from our most intimate moments and the interior of our bodies, out to an audience and into the networked reality of Second Life's multi-user environment, blurring and mixing all of these. This interface, or infolding, begins with the erotic touch of our skin and travels through a network of organs, biological and technological, to create sound in multiple realities. What is required to use it is a sense of one's body, an ability to listen to proprioceptive sensations and a willingness to engage in intimacy. Our hope is to encourage the development of future interfaces that leave behind the expectation of control and move towards co-becoming and intersubjective symbiosis across many shared realities.

---

[66] Haraway, *When Species Meet*, 249.

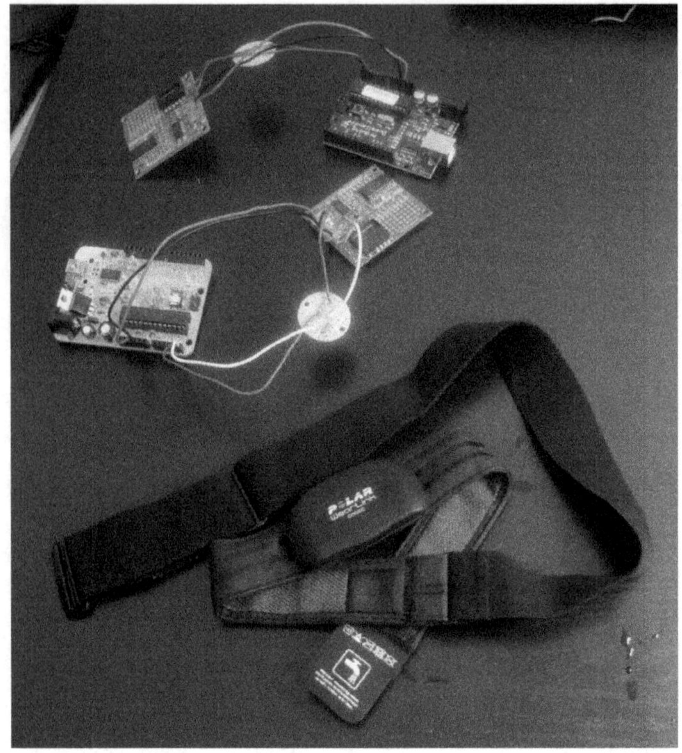

technésexual (2010), Arduino hardware and electrocardiogram chest strap. Photo: Micha Cárdenas and Elle Mehrmand

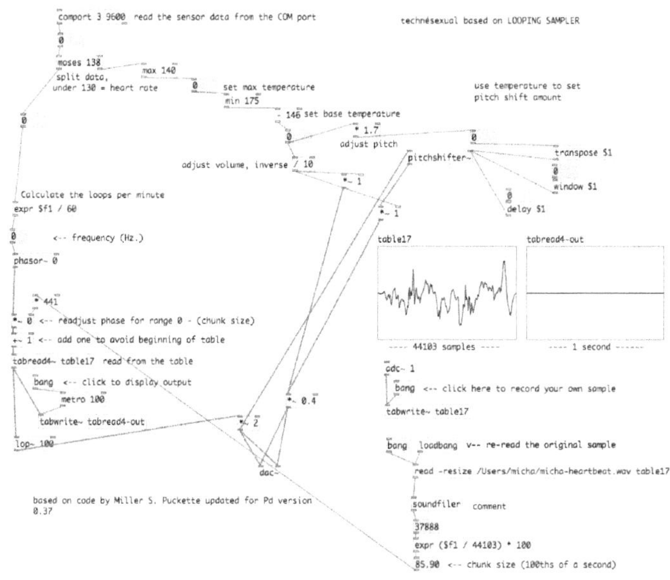

technésexual (2010), Pure Data patch

virus.circus.mem

Micha Cárdenas and Elle Mehrmand

Put on your N95 mask and latex gloves, for your protection and the protection of others.

You walk into a room with a table full of instruments covered in dust, very old instruments from the 2030s, some broken into shards of glass and others burnt. Your study of ancient methods of viral performance art has brought you here to this laboratory in which new ways out of the religious dogma of Western rational science were rediscovered and reinvented. Amidst the collapse of information capitalism, before the myth of rigid national borders was finally eradicated in an instant by the H3N91 mutations, artists experimented with their bodies, applying a Do-It-Yourself and Do-It-Together ethos to medical science to imagine what might lie beyond all they knew.

The sound of your breath is loud inside of the mask. It is unclear what viruses were found here (or not). As you approach a piece of paper on the table half buried under an iridescent dust, the faulty nanoscale photon networks flicker into motion, forming most of an image of an encoded memory, meta-text hovering translucently at an angle above the paper describing the scene.

6.07.37

Our orgasms will burn down their buildings. Once the Chicana Coyotek Gang got us past *la linea*, we were running. We knew that the cambots could tell that we were aroused from our ecg and eeg information data-networks. We trained ourselves to control our heart rates and brain waves so as to be undetected, but the pheromone sensors embedded throughout the city of Les Angeles were sure to track us. We began to run. I've witnessed cambots transfer civils suspicious of being infected to the federal penitentiary where the prison slave labor union now resides. The infected are immediately sentenced to a lifetime of imprisonment, or death if they're lucky. Some are infected with the Rhinovirus, which used to be known as the common cold. If it was so common how bad could it be? There are those of us who question these rhetorics of viruses, and who seek to expose the structures of control that have ripped humanity of a life with pleasure, and instead have given them a life of slavery.

As soon as I saw the lab, my panties were immediately wet. We ran faster so that the lab could shield us, taking us off the grid. I turned my head to catch a swift glimpse of her beautiful eyes; she tried not to look but couldn't resist and gave me a sweet smile. We would always get nervous before our tele-erotic encounters. She flung open the sanitization chamber and we both jumped in. We tore off each other's latex as quick as we could. We have both grown accustomed to enduring the chamber so that we could take off our masks and latex and have haptic sex. I still had to run some tests.

The observers were waiting in the lab as expected. I turned on the bio-audio interface and the ecg data tool. She lay down on the examination table and I plugged her in. She was wearing the conductive-thread metal-detecting dress that we had crafted for this experiment. I chose the first examination tool: the slippery metal njoy. I began to tease her body with the shiny toy. As I touched different parts of her bluetooth dress, the audio changed in pitch, allowing me to aurally parse the data for diagnosis. I had to slide the luscious silver device up and down her body for at least ten minutes before I could hear accurate readings of her information patterns. This aural test is the preliminary foreplay test in which I find out if she has been infected or not.

She passes. I look at her endearingly and get the lube syringe. I spread open those gorgeous legs and insert the syringe in her anal pussy to prep her. She's all lubed up and ready to go. I go to my utensil tray and pick up the same njoy that I used before. I apply lube to the slippery metal and I let the device push through. She starts using circular tantric breathing to focus her breath. I continue to bang her, and as I thrust my hand back and forth my motion-sensitive glove communicates to my strap-on vibrator to give me an amazing pulse of vibration. The faster I thrust, the more pulses my wet clit receives. She is now ready for the glowing glass probe. I generously pour the silky lubrication onto the tip of the glowing phallic wonder, and begin to slide it in her anal pussy. Her R-R intervals change with this larger probe, allowing me to find her interior and hear her within this new intimate perception. The tele-erotic encounter comes to an end and I help her sit up. We exit the lab, leaving the observers to find their own bodies.

The photon networks run out of fuel from the tiny bit of amino acids still in the paper, and the image flickers out. Aware again of your physical safety, you see a bit of glass on your latex glove and step back quickly, shaking it off. Your breath is hot and smelly now, the fear mobilizing chemical compounds in your saliva, thanks to inherited evolutionary mechanisms. Responding to your step, a table is showered in the cold blue of overhead LEDs, with nothing on it but a single clean sheet of paper. Stepping up to it, you rest your hands on the edge of the table. Everything around you spins for a moment; you see artifacts in your eye, though this used to be called seeing stars. The slight tingle above your right ear reminds you of the obsolete technology of neural interfaces as a scene unfolds before your eyes and the voice of the person remembering speaks into your ears.

She's testing me now. My heartbeats are spread open across the screens. The graph jumps up and down with my breath as she moves her instrument up and down my body, connecting the conductive thread, the low droning pitch modulating over the repeating sound of our recorded voices "testing for viral contamination." I breathe more heavily, in and out in a circle through my cock, my stomach, my heart, neck and third eye, activating my body for her, preparing for the next phase of testing. Lying on the operating table, I manage to slip open her zipper to reveal her nipple. I know that she knows, but she stays firm in her mission; we must learn about our bodies to escape the control of those who claim to know better than we do.

Still, holding her dom grip firm, she leans over to move her instrument over a far part of my body, teasing me with her nipple just above my mouth. . . . She lubes me up, placing her electronic gloved hand on my eager ass. Once she thinks I'm ready, she slips it in me and the looped voices change their pitch instantly as my heart rate jumps.. . . .

The heart rate variability comparison data fluctuates wildly across the color spectrum, the voices multiply, the bass reverberates. All I can do is pound my head back against the table, grab the edges and breathe, my mouth quivering through the breathy moan.

Again the scene spins, you feel the tingle above the straps holding your mask on and you're back in the lab. Confused, you're breathing deep now, and with your heart beating loudly in your ears you walk around to the other side of the table with the instruments. An e-reader presents a 3-dimensional image of two women facing each other, black masks on, one woman's hands wrapped around the other's neck, a colorful avatar writhing in the background. The sound of two voices alternating reading sentences is heard.

We are creating femme disturbance. Our corsets, thigh-high stockings, metal sex toys and finely crafted glass dildos are not necessary for capitalist production and feminized immaterial labor, and their presence disturbs the rational drive of the work ethic that demands that we sacrifice our desires during a time of crisis. Our desire for each other's femme bodies is in excess of the rhetorics of medical control. Our desire to see each other naked exceeds the laws preventing us from doing so.

Our queer femme expression disturbs the rigid masculinist structures of science, medicine and capital. Together, we are engaging in femme science to develop new modes of knowledge outside of the limited strictures of corporate-driven medicine, using our desire and cheap handmade electronics to create our own medicine, to learn about our bodies outside of the bounds of our hetero-patriarchal world. Using biometric monitors, instead of quantification and distanced observation, we create a deeper intimacy with each other, moments of interdependence and intersubjectivity. We have inherited a world with thousands of years of science and thought shaped primarily by men[67], where queer and femme knowledge has been viscously stamped out by Western medicine[68], and yet the very time and space we inhabit

---

[67] Elizabeth Grosz, *Time Travels: Feminism, Nature, Power*, annotated edition. (Duke University Press Books, 2005), 165. In "The Time of Thought" Grosz relies heavily on Irigaray for this claim.

[68] Subrosa, *Yes Species*. (Pittsburgh and Chicago, Sabrosa Books,

are not the same as theirs[69], so now we will create our own
worlds of knowledge with our bodies. Femme here is an affect
more than an emotion; it is a combination of sensations and
desires that drives us. We are inspired by Lisa Duggan and
Kathleen McHugh's call for a "femme science [that] is
addressed to the future, a future where femininity as we know it
('normal,' ego-less, tolerant of, and therefore complicit with
deception) will have been completely superceded."[70] We are
pulling these future realities into our own and letting the
resulting disturbances to the laws of physics multiply and
proliferate.

Our fashion will tear apart the established order. Literally
and figuratively, we reappropriate the objects of clothing which
are thought to make up femininity, buying them from sex shops
and then deconstructing them, cutting them open, rewiring them
with our own conductive thread and sensors to create new queer
modes of sexual connection and expression. We buy panties,
bras, thigh-highs and choke collars to turn them into new DIY

2005), accessed January 5, 2012,
http://www.refugia.net/yes/yeschapters.html
[69] Judith Halberstam, *In a Queer Time and Place: Transgender
Bodies, Subcultural Lives* (New York: New York University
Press, 2005), 4.
[70] Lisa Duggan and Kathleen McHugh, "A Fem(me)inist
Manifesto," in *Brazen Femme: Queering Femininity*, ed. Chloe
Brushwood Rose and Anna Camilleri (Arsenal Pulp Press,
2003), 165-170.

sex toys: an ultrasonic rangefinder bra, a pressure-sensing choking collar, a touch-sensitive dress and a motion-sensitive glove that controls a strap-on vibrator. By reconstructing the meaning of science, medicine, femme, love and community we can survive in a world of biopolitical power out of control, a world that tries to kill us every day.

The voices stop. By now you are so disturbed that you run towards the door to escape the myriad of possible infections in this space. Suddenly you are stopped by text hovering inside the door, seeming to block your way for a moment.

virus.circus follows the viral as a transversal line of inquiry that intersects with the militarization of medical authority, microscopic transnational migrations and global economic inequality. Consisting of an episodic series of performances using wearable electronics, soft sensors and live audio to bridge virtual and physical spaces, the performances explore queer futures of latex sexuality and DIY medicine amidst a speculative world of virus hysteria. The history of queer politics shows that the rhetoric of viruses such as HIV is used to control marginalized populations, while viruses such as H1N1 reproduce these structures of power.

You run out and find your body

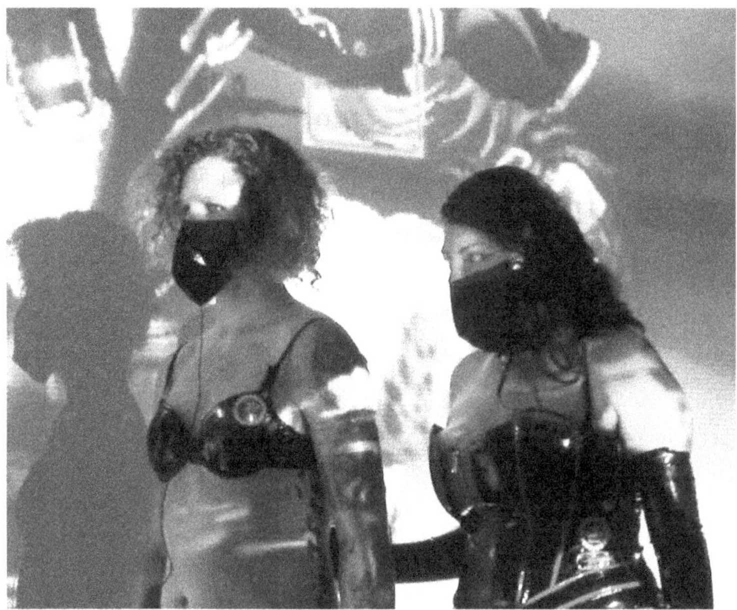

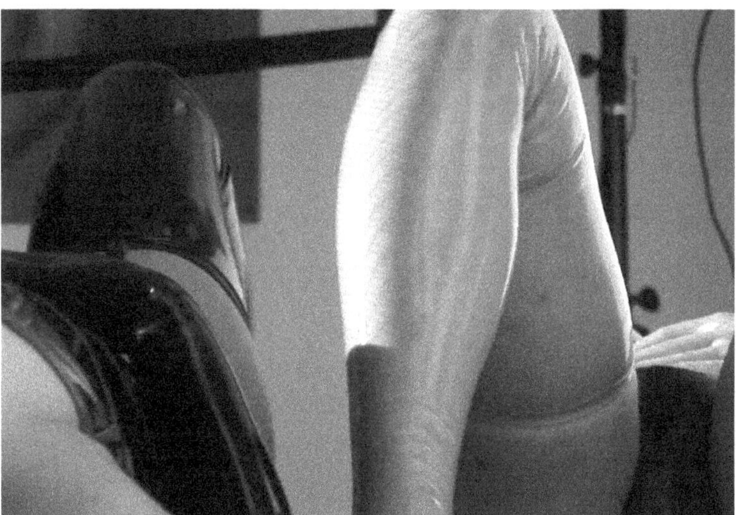

virus.circus.breath (2010), Museum of Contemporary Art, San Diego,
Photo: Ash Smith

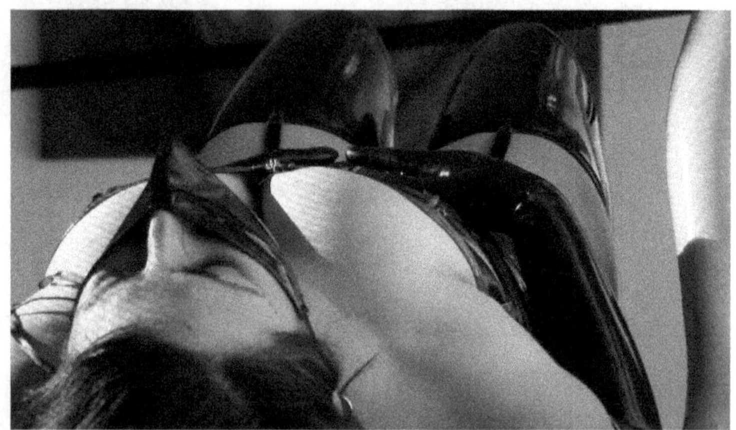

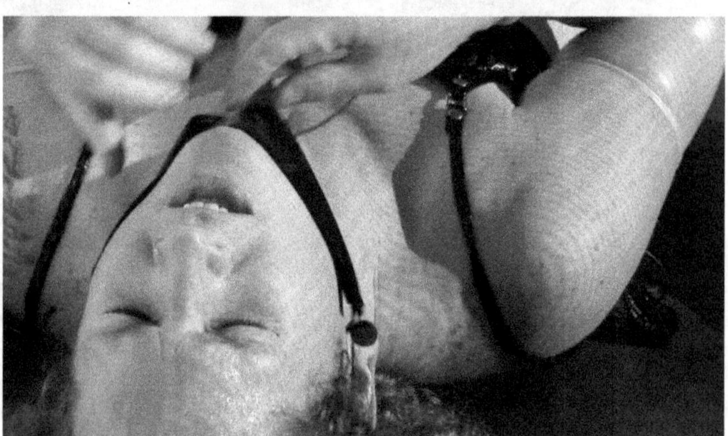

virus.circus.breath (2010), Museum of Contemporary Art, San Diego, Photo: Ash Smith

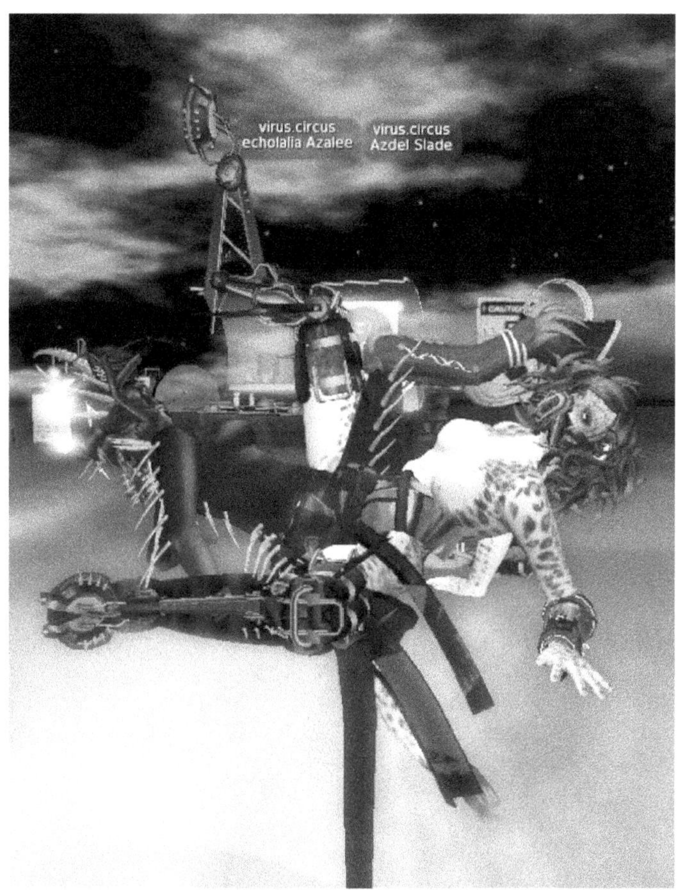

virus.circus.breath (2010), Aztlan Island in Second Life

Becoming Dragon

Homage to orlan, biochemical poetry, a beginning

Avital Ronell says that drugs "split[] existence into
incommensurable articulations."
What drug could this be more true for than administered
hormones?
Foucault speaks of epistemological splits that are true splits after
which the original mode of thinking is inaccessible.
And Jane Gallop writes of woman as the knowing subject,
reconfiguring knowledge.
I commit this transversal act
blurring art and life, for the audience and for myself.
If Guattari was serious about becoming woman, why did he not
use his body as an experimental plateau?
In thanks to Kate Bornstein, in honor of experimentation and
becoming a
more frightening monster than they even expected . . .
Writing the body, not of woman, but of the gender insurgent . . .
I'm so happy to join the dinner party with Cameron the T888,
the sixes
and countless other of Donna's cyborgs,
and other bioengineered beings.
(of course we're all cyborg, I'm just beginning to embrace it)
I take this pill,
and become something else.
June 27, 2008

notes on psychoneuroendocrinology

Today is my first day on estradiol, a pill form of estrogen.

After breakfast, I lay in bed, trying to nap,

I looked at my room in a new way,

saw new things I have never noticed,

the shine of the gears on our bikes,

the red of the curtain shining on the white stripes of the sheet

we hung to block the light,

I listened to sounds far away,

feeling a bit like Anne Rice's newly born vampire,

with new senses, or senses that feel new at least.

Now I'm sure that there's some component,

or a big component,

that is just me being hyper aware, expecting change,

but I feel different already.

I'm reluctant to even say it,

to sound like I'm overstating it,

to sound just crazy,

but this feeling I have, all over, especially in the muscles in my

face,

is not just in my head.

I'm full of excitement

at the potential for change.

I want to ride my bike and feel my body.

I want to take a shower and rub the water off of my skin.

It comes and goes, after the dog park, it wasn't so strong,

there's a slight feeling of nausea too, reminding me that it is a

drug.

Last night my friend warned me that birth control pills make her

nauseous too.

Almost all day I remembered to speak at the top of my voicebox,

and my eyebrows want to sit higher on my face,

all around my eyes, my muscles feel awake.

Cixous said that woman must write woman's body as an

insurgent act,

can we imagine constructing and shape-shifting as a kind of

writing,

and therefore as a kind of insurgency?

Perhaps the trans person must write their hormones,

as a transversal act.

While I don't think I'm becoming woman,

I'm full of joyful excitement for what I am becoming.

Everything is new.

June 28, 2008

notes on psychoneuroendocrinology, 100mg spironolactone

what does 100mg of spironolactone feel like?
it feels like i'm not confident about anything,
grad school, my project, my body, my choices, this.
it's scary to even admit that feeling, to anyone,
scary and also dangerous, for a trans person to admit any doubt.

what combination of chemicals move what part of my body to
create a
sensation of confidence?
it feels like i'm tired all the time.
i try to think about what i'm feeling,
and i think maybe i'm depressed?
i feel constantly reflective,
sensitive to every tiny movement inside myself . . .

"The research of Verhaeghen and colleagues shows when people
are in a reflective mode, they may become more creative,
depressed, or both. Previous research shows that when people
are in a ruminating mode, they are more likely to be depressed,
he said.

"If you think about stuff in your life and you start thinking
about it again, and again, and again, and you kind of spiral away
in this continuous rumination about what's happening to you and

to the world—people who do that are at risk for depression," he
said."

in *Carnal Art: Orlan's Refacing* by C. Jill O'Bryan, I read

> Orlan substitutes her body for language so that she performs
> this fiction as though a live signifier; shifting shape, her face
> does not literally articulate a fixed identity: "I make myself
> into a new image in order to produce new images."
> Derrida's term *auto-affection*—a substitute for self-
> presence, that which, he claims, we can never purely
> know—comes closest to describing human experience at
> this level. . . . Auto-affection is the state of giving-oneself-a-
> presence. . . . Derrida writes: ". . . Hearing oneself speak is
> not the interiority of an inside that is closed in upon itself; it
> is the irreducible openness in the inside; it is the eye and the
> world within speech. Phenomenological reduction is a
> scene, a theater stage."

Can I write this? What does it mean to engage in this process of
reflecting
on the changing chemistry in my body,
which makes me feel something else?

"Much like the paradigms installed by the discovery of
endorphins, Being-on-drugs indicates that a structure is already

in place, prior to the production of that materiality we call drugs,
including virtual reality or cyberprojections."
— Avital Ronell, *Crack Wars*

Finally a cloudy cold day in San Diego.
Riding my bike I'm so grateful for the cold wind.
The light is blue-gray, instead of the usual yellow pounding
socal sun.
It's a bit more like how I feel.
I'm happy to feel something,
even if it's feeling a little fucked up, like Ariana's cow,
but her poems are so much better than this one.
I hear Sarah McLaughlin's *Adia* ˆand feel cliché,
even though I remember crying to this song,
heartboken over that blonde girl with the sun-faded neck tattoo
in miami.
A friend of mine told me that her transgirl roommate would cry
and cry.
I feel much more still, listening,
waiting for change, looking down at my breasts,
like a 14-year-old girl,
trying to eat a lot, hoping for them to grow.
smiling in the mirror, seeing if i look cuter that way, more
feminine?
maybe i'm just too fucking self-absorbed.

notes on becoming, 2mg estradiol

how quickly things are new

is that just the estrogen talking?

she says and buries her head in the pillow.

it's amazing how fast things turn around,

in just a week

i feel things for her that i can barely describe

and i'm afraid of the words that do want to come out.

after so much sweat and saliva and groaning

she says she's afraid

for my health

she finally researched my meds

and she's worried about me

and she's worried that i'll become someone else

that she's falling in love with someone who's disappearing.

i wish i had an answer

i don't.

i am becoming someone else

but aren't we all?

always becoming

creating false labels for moments

that we're outgrowing as we speak them

learning, creating, building, slipping into our new selves

every moment?

position is an illusion, thinking of bergson in bed

but position is also an orgasm, which is not so illusory

i said to a guy at a party

have you ever met someone who turns everything in your whole
life upside down

who changes everything?

i didn't know he just showed up because he heard the music

and then as he hesitated to reply i got pulled back onto the dance
floor

she says through her tears that she gets it

she's always checked the other box for ethnicity

and always thought there shouldn't even be a box,

i just look at her as she says it

in a moment of wet motion, tears and hair in her eyes,

and a moment of slow, painful, longing movement

in myself and everywhere in the world

between questions now and answers then

THIS MEDICATION IS A PINK, ROUND, TABLET,
SCORED IMPRINTED WITH M ON ONE SIDE AND E 4 ON
THE OTHER SIDE

are you going to move with me in june?

        but what is going to happen to your body, and your brain?

i just can't take this vague ambiguity in our relationship any
more

        i just feel like i'm going to be pushed to the side in the future

        we need you to move your office to the new space . . .

where are you going to live in january? you know you could stay
                                        here if you want to . . .
what city do you want to move to?

            i'm just afraid that you're going to break my heart.

if you loved me you would want to move with me.

                    aren't you going away in the summer?

it all seems too far away, so many variables, so many desires, so
many questions, how could i possibly know what i'm going to
do, if i barely even know what i want to do? i can only think a
few weeks ahead, and i know that everything is about to change,
and i'm so happy that it is, but i feel something like sylvia
plath's impending train wreck, gestating, birthing, walking into
the unknown, terrifying and wonderful . . .

so satisfied with the simple certainty of a bobby pin, a wet kiss
and a long orgasm, anything more seems like wild speculation.

notes on becoming, a bathroom mirror

coming out of the stall

rushing out of the bathroom

i glance back at the mirror for an instant

and i see a girl's face

and i stop

and look back again.

i'm leaving work in a hurry to get back to the lab at school,

i've been crying, the office was empty and i was sending

emails to a lover about our changing relationship,

so maybe my eyes are puffy, softer,

i pause and look in the mirror

and wonder if i can see a girl in that face

again

and hope that i may someday

but there's a way that you can look at a face closely

and the gender slips away.

sometimes when i look at pictures of trans people i try to look at

their faces and see their birth gender, i think its an internalized

transphobic habit i still have,

but sometimes i look at cisgender people's faces and think they

look trans

and wonder if they're just passing really well

or if i'm just so gender dysphoric (or euphoric) that i can't even

see gender "right"

there is so much activity, in that act of seeing,

that is outside conscious thought and words,

the world shifts and pulses in front of the naked eye

as it is held open.

but right now, in this bathroom, it's late, no one's going to come

in

and i look femme-y today, so it should be safe,

i adjust my bag strap and look into my own eyes

and wonder if amidst all this hurry,

there's a girl in the middle, emerging,

if all the people who call me man, guy, dude, he, mister,

might someday see me as something else.

someday soon.

but sometimes i don't even care,

and those are times that matter,

passing moments in the bedroom,

sitting in bed talking,

walking past the mirror,

laughing in the bathroom.

because the people who love me and who i love

can see me for what i am

and that is not a man

and not a woman

but maybe a girl

and maybe something else.

a series of micro-transitions

maybe we can think of transition as

a series of micro-transitions

daily decisions and events that change us, ever so slightly

the decision to grow your hair out, or to change the way you

wear it,

shopping for different jeans, shoes, bracelets.

they rush into the airport, with a few minutes to spare

and try to grab a beer and some nachos,

the waitress walks up and says "what can i get you ladies."

walking out to a bar at night, crossing the street, some

male fuckhead unaware of his own privilege yells

something about sluts at us as he drives by,

or boarding the plane back home, the stewardess says

"sir, um, miss, can you put your laptop under the seat,"

while we try to get Circus Linux to work on the in-seat game

console.

she tries out base for the first time, Smartshade from Clairol is

what L uses,

so it's okay that their skin colors are different,

it has some uncanny ability to match the shade of your face,

once you rub it in.

the base works, looking a bit softer, maybe, and less stubbly,

hopefully.

they meet up with old friends at a bar in the mission,

BAR shining in bright red neon in the window,

and Rae says she looks great.

there must be nano-transitions as well, only visible through

advanced technologies,

imperceptible shifts and rotations of neurochemicals.

the moments of change are small events, which

they point out to each other after they happen, laughing and

feeling happy about them,

sharing tiny moments of transformation which are so huge,

resonating across a series of events, changing the meaning of all

of them,

the unknown unfolding through micro-events,

refracting the color of the previous and future events into

different hues, shades and gradations.

Inbetween names

if liminal space is the space in between two worlds, states,
bodies,
then i entered another kind of liminal space today.
we got up late, i woke up excited to change my name,
but i was upset that L didn't want to get up.
i read it wrong, thinking she didn't really want to go with me.
i tell her this over our americanos at our favorite coffee place,
and she almost cries, saying how happy she is to come with me,
saying how sad it always makes me when i have to show
someone my ID
and she almost makes me cry too, but then we get our bagels and
rush out.
in the line at the courthouse there's a loud crazy guy,
in a nice coat and mirrored glasses, but with baggy jeans and
sneakers.
he keeps laughing too loud and calling the tellers mommy,
saying:
"mommy, you're a nice person."
he finally finishes his filing and walks out saying "i'm the
district attorney,"
and laughing all the way down the hall.
the first teller, where you buy the forms, shows me two packets
and asks which i want

their titles are NAME CHANGE FORM PACKET and NAME
AND GENDER CHANGE FORM PACKET.

she just shows them to me, apparently she can't say the names.

but in this state you can only file to change your gender after
bottom surgery,

so i take the NAME CHANGE FORM PACKET.

the teller has a nice shirt with wolves on it,

we laugh and hold hands standing at the teller together,

probably looking like the married couples that usually fill out
these name change forms.

afterwards, i have to call the local newspaper to file a classified
ad announcing my name change,

in case any interested persons want to come to the hearing in 4
weeks and disagree,

on the phone, i tell them my name is micha, and stumble saying
it,

even though this has been my name for years now,

thinking about which name on the form they're looking at.

i give them the billing name on my credit card, my legal name,

in the conversation i have both names and neither.

for the next 6 weeks i'm inbetween names.

Gender and Desire in Virtual Worlds,
Conversation with
Allucquére Rosanne Stone, Ph.D.

MC: Part of why I wanted to do this performance *Becoming Dragon* is to see how we could develop new genders outside of male and female, to see if we can use virtual environments to create new genders that are not restricted to male or female. Sometimes people propose gender as a spectrum as a more radical notion, but I am proposing, or as the book *Genderqueer: Voices from Beyond the Sexual Binary* proposes, gender can be unrestricted by the male/female binary, some people describe their gender as zombie or a bunny or a dragon, and other people think that gender is kind of an expressive texture. So each person can construct their own gender on a daily basis and I think that the first time I said this to you, you said that gender is an object of power, or function of power and that maybe creating new genders is not possible or not useful?

ARS: Gender insofar as we know the word in Western, developed society—and I'm talking primarily about the cultures I know—United States, Europe, Middle East, Asia—is something that joins us in a power structure. Part of the problem with talking about gender outside a power structure is we never see it outside of a power structure, because you can never get outside of a power structure. We're always in some kind of a power structure, and that has to do with the way we choose to live within the frameworks that we live; we're always within some framework of power, some warp field.

My view on this—which I'm willing to change based on evidence—is that outside of a power structure the concept of gender would be absolutely meaningless, because gender as we know it in Western society exists to serve a power structure. You always need somebody on the down side. Gender is constructed in that way, so that one group of people can gain a particular kind of pleasure that they do from being a in a one-up, one-down power situation. And for reasons I am not entirely clear we have linked gender so firmly to the idea of power so I don't know where people have seen in any other way.

So really pause there for a moment because I don't think that you really agree with me and I want to discuss it.

MC: I see what you're saying, that gender supports the existing culture that we find ourselves, that gender is a function of power, but I wonder about the idea of subcultures, or the idea that power is heterogeneous. We're not always in the same power structures all the time, or as affected by the power structures. Think of going to a queer club, or lesbian bars. I would think we experience gender's relationship to power differently in that situation, than, say, at work, or at school. Maybe in a place like Second Life, we also have a different experience of power. Do you think that's true?

ARS: Yes, I think that our experience of almost anything interpersonally changes depending upon where we are, and I think I said in the *War of Desire and Technology* that you're never the same person to the mail deliverer that you are to your lover, except in the situation in which the mail deliverer is your lover. And Jay has just commented here, "And even then!"

MC: You wrote a lot about your experience of transitioning in the *Neovagina Monologues*. Much of what my writing about transition deals with is the notion of becoming something else and someone else, and wanting to resist essentialism, or wanting to not be tied to the notion that I am something that I will permanently be and I can't become something else. But that's hard for people, like for people that are close to me. I think that people like to think that there is some true self.

ARS: I can be pretty definitive about that from my point of view, I don't think there is such a thing as a true self. I think that can be seen as a curse, but in fact it's a gift. I think we have the opportunity to put on and take off identities, within the limits that our society puts on us because of course our society fights that, bitterly. A fair amount of our lives are spent fighting our society's attempt to identify us, and limit us.

The sequence of identity does not converge, Peter Allen said that everything old is new again, and I think that all those apply to the idea of identity, in a playful way, which is the way I very much like to address it.

MC: We crashed again, but I just turned off the motion tracking and head capture and we're back and should be more stable on this end.

ARS: The crashing is part of it. We all feel like we're back in 1980. Technology is really not that good.

MC: I want to ask about the notion of the way fantasy bleeds into reality and the question of how if we wanted to try to use Second Life or virtual environments to learn new ways of being or walking, or new genders, we think there is some kind of bleed between fantasy and our real selves. Some people argue that fantasy is just fantasy, and it's safe to do what you want in fantasy without worrying about how it affects your real life. Whereas some people, for example antiporn feminists, would say looking at porn trains people to think that women are objects. Others think that fantasy is not necessarily safe or distinct from our everyday lives.

ARS: There's a lot of opportunity for interpreting what the hell gender means. It's important to remember that ultimately we're talking about real people stuck in real bodies and who experience real oppressions, as a result of their positionality. You can't get away from positionality; everybody lives somewhere and everybody is subject to some power structure. I keep coming back to that because I do worry about the idea of gender floating away into the ether. I think gender play is really great and I think everybody should do it. On the other hand, I think that when you do that you have to keep in mind that gender means differently depending where you are, and what situation you are in and what society you are in. Gender has social and cultural meanings that are rooted in reality, that affect both reality and virtual reality. They are coupled together and the thing that couples them together is the human body. We are the things that mediate between the virtual and the physical.

I don't want to be talking in multiple perspectives at the same time, even though I am. I'm clearly a trans-y, I have chosen to transition. I made the hard choice to have surgery, so I have stakes in this as well. On the other hand, I have lots of friends who do gender play and don't feel they have to put their bodies on the line, and I support that 100 percent. I don't think that going down the surgery route is necessarily for everybody. The thing is, I need to go back and talk about what gender means and how gender means. We can talk about how gender means in a group of friends, in an isolated situation where everyone is more or less consenting and we are able to wall ourselves off from the larger world. But if we are not walling ourselves off from the larger world, if we are living in the world we are thereby implicitly accepting standards of the way power works around us. In other words, if we are performing gender out on a city street, say, then we will find that society will impose itself on us, whether we want it to or not, and that's where the rubber hits the road!

If you want to perform whatever gender you want to perform, and you try it in downtown Riyadh, you might find the circumstance works to your disadvantage. If you want to do it in Santa Cruz, California, it might be a whole different kind of show. Any way you do it, you are subjecting yourself to a preexisting structure and that's my main point. When we say gender is an infinite field of play, I think that's fine. You can say that, I can say that, we can all maintain that, right up until the minute when some bigot comes up to us with an empty wine bottle and hits us over the head. Then we bleed, and the rubber is on the road. Jake says, "Then I take back the wine bottle and hit him over the head, and then we are both engaged in life." I just want to make sure that we keep all those alternatives in mind, that's all.

MC: On this notion of positionality, I know we're talking about material reality and the way that we have gender placed on us and we receive violence because of that gender, but I wonder also about this idea of being in transition, because I think that, if we think about Henri Bergson or Massumi then we could think that these positions that we're choosing are not so clear. They are in flux all the time. They are changing in the way we perform and the way we perceive them. We can think that there is a position that we choose and we receive consequences for, but I think that position is illusory. The position is always changing depending not only on what we perform but on who we are standing in front of.

ARS: Boy I'm having fun playing devil's advocate, let me tell you. I titled my book *The War of Desire,* and this is what we're talking about. Let's talk about the part that applies here. We are free to do whatever we want, insofar as we are able to get away with it. But as soon as we place ourselves in proximity to a societal power structure, then we are going to be living our lives in opposition to that structure, or we can choose to accept that structure. It just happens that because the issue of gender is so explosive in Western society that if we choose the field of gender in which to have this discussion, then we are taking a position which is quite charged. Because as you know, as much as we may believe identities change all the time—and they should—still, when we find ourselves in the presence of almost any societal structure, that societal structure works to prevent that from happening, because it's inimical to power structures. So what I'm saying is *you forget that at your peril.* Because if you forget that society, every society or every one we're likely to encounter, will work to stabilize gender, then we have to think that keeping gender fluid is a task, it's an activity, and it needs to be continually done. It never happens on its own. Gender will never be fluid unless you continually work to make it fluid. Because when you stop making it fluid, your society's structure will move right in and collapse that field into some gender. Very much like friction stopping objects in motion, yes, I was thinking of the quantum mechanical of collapsing things, but yes. . . .

Society has inertia. Society works like a field in which it imparts inertia to you, and the task of trying to avoid that inertia is one that never stops.

Editor's note: This panel's audio recording contained multiple layers of distortion and included numerous software crashes, so this text is a rough translation, at best.

The Body in Transmission / Transition, Learning to Live in Mixed Realities: Conversation with Stelarc

MC: About this notion of "The Body in Transmission / Transition"—the idea seems like a strong link between your work and my own. For example, your project *Ping Body*, where your body was responding to network calls from the audience. You can explain more about that. I'm interested in this question of how we think about the body as something that is constantly changing, evolving, becoming obsolete and dying away right before our eyes.

S: I think the idea of the body as an extended operational system is what happens when we function with mixed realities. The body now, to perform effectively in the televisual world that it is in, needs to perform with mixed realities and needs to interface with both physical and virtual spaces. In doing so, the body is constantly being reconfigured, reconstructed. The body ebbs and flows from the twilight of real life into the midnight of Second Life.

To see the body as purely a biological construct immersed in a local space and bounded with skin is not really adequate anymore.

MC: When I was in your gallery in Second Life the other day I was looking at a photo of the *Ping Body* performance and in that you were wearing some sort of visor. Could you say a little more about that performance?

S: I did a series of Internet performances. The initial one was titled *Fractal Flesh*,and that occurred with my body in Luxembourg, and people in the Pompidou Center in Paris, the media lab in Helsinki, the Doors of Perception conference in Amsterdam were able to access my body and remotely control it using a muscle stimulation system. In that case, in that performance, I had a heads-up display enabling me to see the person who was programming me. There was a kind of intimacy without proximity, a kind of intimacy without skin contact.

Ping Body was a little different in that instead of people in other places, the body becomes a kind of barometer for Internet activity. In other words, the body is moving depending on the rate of ping signals coming back to the host computer. That depended crudely on the amount of Internet activity. The body here becomes a crude barometer of Internet activity. It was more an exposing of the Internet structure.

Whereas a further performance that we did over the Net called *Parasite* involved a customized search engine that scans the Internet, finds images of bodies on the Internet, displays them to my heads-up helmet, and the JPEG file is analyzed and depending on the size of the file and the complexity of the file my body moves in a certain way, involuntarily. In this case, the body moves to the images it sees which have been harvested from the World Wide Web.

They were the three different kinds of performances that involved remotely activating the body. I was really interested in the idea, Azdel, of the body performing involuntarily and in fact performing as a kind of a split body. The body partly being able to perform with its own intuitive agency but also half of its body prompted by people in other places. I call this, especially this experience of a distributed body and a split body, as "fractal flesh." In other words, bodies and bits of bodies spatially separated but electronically connected with the Internet as a kind of crude external nervous system for the body.

MC: In that performance there's already some form of this idea of mixed realities, where in your heads-up display you're seeing something different than you're experiencing with the rest of your body in your physical location. Pyewacket (last name?) was showing me your gallery and some of your work in Second Life. As I said in the beginning, I like this notion of mixed realities because it seems to me to imply, just the mixed notion, has a kind of messiness where we're not privileging one reality and saying that it's virtual or real but instead, it's a combination, a constant interplay. I'm interested in Second Life because I feel like it brings to the fore a lot of issues that are already issues in everyday life. We're constantly dealing with different realities: the reality of the body, of emotions, of ideas, or the person we're talking to on our cell phone or texting with. In Second Life this split is highlighted. Do you want to say more about what you're doing with Second Life or why you find it interesting?

S: Well I think that idea of not privileging one particular form of operation, whether it's real life or Second Life… what's interesting for me is the interface or what happens between real life and Second Life or between one augmented reality that might be locally performed and one that might be tele-operated in a remote space. I think the notion of mixed realities is important because it's the only way that we can function effectively in a high-tech terrain of fast and powerful and precise machines and instruments. Our biological metabolism is far too wet and soft and imprecise. It needs to be augmented not only with machines but with other avatars from other places, with artificial entities.

It is important that we see, it's a strange time in which we are living, in fact. We can now indefinitely preserve a cadaver with plasternation while simultaneously we can sustain a comatose body on a life support system. We have cryogenically preserved bodies awaiting reanimation in the future. We're constructing partially living entities in vitro. The blood in my body might be circulating in your body at some time in the future. An organ extracted from one body is exchanged and implanted into another body. All of that is already happening in real life, and that's not to even mention the transmission and transformative possibilities and the kind of fluidity of form and identity that occurs with the body and its avatars in Second Life.

MC: All of this thinking about death makes me think of one more question before we go to the audience for questions. The notion of learning to live is definitely part of my project that I'm doing now, thinking about training and ways that we try to change ourselves and become something else and learn to live in a different way. You said before we started the panel that you had hoped that you could use that third arm that your avatar is wearing, your *Third Hand* project in real life, for much longer than you were able to. It seems like you've done a lot of this, trying to experiment with learning to live in new ways.

S: The way I see these possibilities is that they are ones of Alternate Anatomical Architectures. These could be bodies with additional arms, mechanical arms or limbs. The body might be a body with an extra ear—for example, we're now surgically constructing an ear on my arm, an ear that would become an Internet-enabled organ in any Wi-Fi hotspot. You'll be able to listen in to what my ear is hearing wherever you are and wherever I am. But these Alternate Anatomical Architectures aren't about machines or bodies only, they are also about Azdel's *Becoming Dragon*, interfacing the body and its machines with artificial entities and avatars that allow us to function remotely and to function beyond the boundaries of our skin and to experience the world in alternate sensory modes. I would characterize even what's happening in Second Life as an Alternate Anatomical Architecture where the body performs, in a way, best as its avatar. I have a statement about the fact that avatars have no organs. An avatar is a hollow body, a body that doesn't need a biological organ structure. Our organs, in fact, are badly designed and inadequate for living longer than about seventy-five years in good health.

MC: Unless you want to go back to those points maybe we can see if there are questions from the audience?

S: It would be great to get questions and see what other people are thinking and feeling about some of the ideas. Especially, I think the other interesting thing with Azdel's performance, and one that's often underestimated, is this idea of immersion. It's only by being immersed for longer periods of time in Second Life that the body will comprehend the problems of functioning effectively in a virtual space.

MC: Does anyone have a question, in real life or Second Life? I can't see you in real life so you'll have to speak up if you're here.

Audience member: It goes back to the body without organs and the avatar. I was thinking, in relation to Stelarc's project with the virtual head that was programmed to converse and respond and the idea of avatars being able to be set free. Something in the

training and then releasing into Second Life as an extension of
self that you no longer control.

S: That's really an interesting possibility, the idea that an avatar
becomes an intelligent agent to the point where it can be
autonomous and in a sense, allowed to inhabit Second Life
without the necessity of guidance from a real-life body. The
project that you're talking about is titled *Prosthetic Head* and it
was initially meant to be an online entity, but in trying to
construct an intelligent agent with real-time lip syncing and
speech synthesis, in the end we had to construct it as more of a
gallery installation rather than a Web presence. I also saw that as
a conversational system. In other words, connected to a real
head, the virtual head would be capable of interesting
conversation and verbal and facial expressions. I think the idea
of constructing avatars that become intelligent agents and
entities in themselves and become autonomous to inhabit Second
Life, that's really an interesting idea.

MC: Somebody has been showing me around a bunch of
artificial intelligence bots around Second Life and we talked to
one Alice bot that was not trained so well, but then I went to
your gallery, Stelarc, and talked to your bot. Pyewacket said you
have been programming it so it had lots of clever answers about
"what is art" and "what is life." This issue makes me think about
the way that saying that the body is imprecise or obsolete is a

provocation. It seems that in all of these years that artificial intelligence technology is still not very good and that what we really need is larger scales of complexity, perhaps. How do you feel about how far it's come?

S: I do feel that that idea of the obsolescence of the body is actually not meant in that we can somehow exist disembodied, or that intelligence somehow would be disembodied. Really, what this means to me is that the body in this form, and with these particular functions, can't adequately cope with the machines and the instruments and the operation, the tele-operation and the surrogate robots and other intelligent entities that it has to function with. To say that the body is obsolete specifically refers to this biological body with this form and with these present functions and its limited parameters of survival. This body is not going to exist much more than seventy-five years in good health.

MC: I asked that person why she was interested in artificial intelligence in Second Life, which I thought was funny because so many people come to Second Life to talk to other people, and she wanted to just come here and talk to programs. She said she was excited about the possibility of these AIs talking to each other and making something new. Something that I think is really interesting is the challenge of really thinking of something new. Maybe if we could train avatars to run off on their own through Second Life, they might do that. I just find Second Life to be an example of how hard it is to think beyond current parameters. Most places I go as this dragon, people say "OMG, a dragon," or "Eek!" or something like that. It seems that most people in Second Life are duplicating a lot of what they see in real life.

S: Well, that's true. I think, on the one hand, it's seductive to mimic or translate real life into Second Life. We shouldn't forget that when we do this translation, something else happens. So even if we want to completely mimic real life, there's going to be some kind of rupture, some kind of slippage that occurs. Even the mimicking of real life can generate some interesting and unexpected occurrences. I think the other way of looking at it is to follow through with this idea that an autonomous intelligent entity, as an avatar, might be capable of emergent behavior, especially in its interactions with other similar entities. Then you would have a kind of meta-reality, an MR, rather than an RL (real life) or SL (Second Life), that is constructed by these autonomous and intelligent entities.

[18:48] Liliann Ling: do you think an avatar is embodied or disembodied?

S: I think an avatar is quite embodied. Firstly, it's embodied as an image or a 3-dimensional model that is the result of some code. It appears on a screen or on a laptop or a monitor that is part of an interconnected global media communication system. No, I think we need to see avatars as embodied. I don't think we should see them as some kind of ephemeral entity, but really one that, as an image, can function in ways that a physical body can't. Avatars don't have to perform in gravity with mass and friction. Of course, sometimes these are simulated in Second Life, but the interesting thing really is, for me, what happens between your avatar and my avatar, between Second Life and real life, between this gendered body and your gendered body, at this particular time or at some future time. I would be really intrigued if we could have some kind of time slippage factored into Second Life, where we might be able to, in real time, pause, replay and reenact something in a better way, or in an alternate way, the idea of multiple worlds of interaction to factor into Second Life.

MC: I kind of have some of that experience watching my life on a ten-second delay for two weeks [in the live video feed from real life to Second Life]. I wanted to say to the person who asked about disembodiment and embodiment that I think that it's not so clear. A big part of what I'm trying to do with this project also is to show the notion of mixed reality is built into our ideas of how we understand the world. Heidegger talks about the idea of *Gestell*, or framework, where we find ourselves in the world in this body and so that's how we imagine things. Then we go to

Second Life and we just make new bodies. I feel like so much of the appeal of Second Life is just that process of imagining yourself in some other body and seeing yourself in another body. The book *Second Person*,[71] that Noah Wardrip-Fruin edited, made this really strong distinction between first person games and third person games like Second Life. In Second Life you don't just walk around shooting things through the eyes of your character. You have this experience of seeing your character all the time. I find that when people play this game, they almost immediately, as soon as they come into the world, they say, "Oh, look at my hair! It looks awful! I have to fix it!" or "I want crazy blue hair," but they immediately have a subtle emotional connection with their avatar, some kind of emotional feedback immediately with this simple idea that "this thing represents me" or "it is me" or "it is a reflection of me."

S: I think too one needs to be careful about this idea of me and my avatar. In a sense it perpetuates a kind of Cartesian split, and I think of course this is almost inevitable when we speak in language because language encourages us to speak as a first

---

[71] Celia Pearce and Artemesia, "Communities of Play: The Social Construction of Identity in Persistent Online Game Worlds," in *Second Person: Role-Playing and Story in Games and Playable Media,* ed. Pat Harrigan and Noah Wardrip-Fruin, (The MIT Press, 2010), 311.

person subject: "I do this" or "I do that" or "me and my avatar." The avatar in a sense becomes a kind of third person. It's me in my head, my body and then my avatar. I think this is a seductive but fallacious way of imagining what's going on. There's nothing other than this body. There's nothing inside this head. On the other hand, something different is happening in Second Life when you're performing as the avatar on screen.

M: I just sent those two questions back to local chat. . . .

[2008/12/08 18:51] Melody Trefusis: Well, Second Life gives people a chance to be someone or something that couldn't never be in Real Life. Do you think it will go further? And how?

S: I think it does allow you to construct your body in ways that you couldn't in real life. I've had a third hand but I've never had a robot arm. I've had the extended arm, but in Second Life I have my robot arm. One thing that I don't have in Second Life that I have in real life at the moment is an extra ear on my arm. It's only a relief of an ear at the moment. The next step is to lift the helix of the ear and grow a soft earlobe. Actually, Pyewacket mentioned that we are working on being able to graft extra ears on any avatar that visits my Second Life site. So if you visit the site you'll be able to undergo an operation that results in an ear on your arm. We're not there yet, but it's something that we want to do.

M: Also, there's this question about overstimulating the body and these kind of body modifications' being kind of unsurvivable or unsustainable?

S: I don't think that you can ever overstimulate the body. I guess I've always thought of prosthetic attachments not as a symptom of lack but rather a sign of excess. With the increasing proliferation of micro-miniaturized technology it will be possible to augment the body's structure with implanted devices or attached machines or to develop some kind of neural implants where you can more efficiently input information and images. I've always dealt with excess rather than sensory deprivation. Having said that, my early performances involved doing sensory deprivation. I spent a week in a gallery where I stitched my eyelids and lips shut with surgical needle and thread and stayed in a gallery without speaking, without eating, without seeing. I could hear. That was the only sense that was available to me. Those early performances were about discovering the general physiological parameters of the body, but simultaneously constructing alternate objects and extensions that have always been in excess. I don't have a mechanical hand because I am an amputee. I have an additional hand, or an extra ear, or a six-legged walking machine, to navigate through the world as some large machine insect architecture.

Imagining New Worlds: Biopolitics and Self-Governance in Second Life

Panel with Micha Cárdenas, Brian Holmes and James Morgan / Rubaiyat Shatner

[15:53] Brianee Hoffnung: The question of who rules us or how are we governing ourselves... seems like the basic issue here

[15:54] Azdel Slade: can u say more brian?

[15:54] Brianee Hoffnung: i mean, beyond the graphics, what's at issue is the intimacy of a life, how it is going to change over time

[15:55] Brianee Hoffnung: while moving through society. I was very impressed by this whole proposal . . . because I thought I understood someone was trying a real existential experiment .

[15:56] Azdel Slade: thanks . . .

[15:56] Conover's Flight-Helper 6.3.3 (WEAR ME!): Flight-helper is ready and operational.

[15:56] Brianee Hoffnung: and that is of the essence

[15:56] IM: Symphony Delicioso: i know im here.. tryin to find out what i missed

[15:56] Azdel Slade: do you think the link between sl and the alter-globalization movement, if we can call it that, in the challenge of creating new worlds, is a fair or interesting link?

[15:57] Brianee Hoffnung: yeah, totally - it's the whole thing imho! sorry this typing is so damn slow by the way!

[15:57] Azdel Slade: -its ok

[15:57] Symphony Delicioso: yes

[15:57] Azdel Slade: im patient, have lots of time

[15:57] Rubaiyat Shatner: is the meaning changed at all by us being in a single corporations playground?

[15:58] Brianee Hoffnung: what else is to be done if not experiment with who you are and can be?

[15:58] Azdel Slade: thats a question i have about sl, or it seems, a real problem - that its run now by one corporation

[15:58] Brianee Hoffnung: we are always in a corporations playground these days, unfortunately

[15:58] Symphony Delicioso: i agree

[15:58] Brianee Hoffnung: one, or two - no big difference

[15:58] Azdel Slade: it seems though, that opensim and realxtend, open source servers...

[15:58] Rubaiyat Shatner: I mean that as I see it we have no rights here, does that have an effect on the worlds we can and do create?

[15:58] Azdel Slade: can offer a more open system like the web

[15:59] Brianee Hoffnung: the question: can we talk with each other anyway? I think we can

[15:59] Feilen Timeless: Linden seems to be highly liberal with how it treats it's users, it's the only way they can profit

[15:59] Brianee Hoffnung: Micha has been sending out very intense signals for years now

[15:59] Rubaiyat Shatner: but frankly you can be silenced (technology aside) for any or no reason

[15:59] Feilen Timeless: *linden labs

[15:59] Rubaiyat Shatner: and no recourse

[16:00] Azdel Slade: brian, you said something that passed by

[16:00] Brianee Hoffnung: sorry Rubiyat I am too slow to really participate - but can a human being be silenced by anything except death?

[16:01] Azdel Slade: about experimenting with who and what u can be being important

[16:01] Brianee Hoffnung: what I mean is, yes there are rules

[16:01] Azdel Slade: thats like guattari's ethico-aesthetic paradigm right, of creating the self as a political act

[16:01] YaoChi Zhangsun: To a degree by various forms of muzzling people can be silenced short of death

[16:01] Brianee Hoffnung: but those rules can always be broken, or bypassed, there are always other meda

[16:01] Rubaiyat Shatner: well an avatar can be silenced within world, but I get your meaning

[16:02] Azdel Slade: but aside from silenced, linden labs creates the conditions of possibility by controlling the servers

[16:02] Brianee Hoffnung: it is a problem, that an avatar can be silenced

[16:02] Azdel Slade: and its as simple as clicking the mute button on them for anyone to do

[16:02] Feilen Timeless: There is a theoretical problem, but no real problem unless LL gets taken over

[16:03] Brianee Hoffnung: but getting murdered by the police like Alexander Grigoporolous in Greece is another issue

[16:03] Azdel Slade: true, so can there be biopolitics in sl without a body and death? or, do things here matter at all? sure, i think there r degrees...

[16:04] YaoChi Zhangsun: solitary incarceration is serious too

[16:04] Brianee Hoffnung: I would focus on what can be done, which is a tremendous artistist expression. To answer: when there is expression, there is biopolitics. I am very interested in how this expressive force can be used

[16:05] Azdel Slade: to clarify for people, i think of biopolitics as a politics of everyday life or the struggle for control over our daily lives

[16:05] Symphony Delicioso: thank you for clarifying

[16:05] Azdel Slade: do u guys agree?

[16:06] Brianee Hoffnung: and damn the rules by the way! - indeed, the question is who could really rule one's daily life

[16:06] YaoChi Zhangsun: Sounds rather Libertarian in terms of folks being in control of their own lives

[16:06] Rubaiyat Shatner: it makes sense

[16:06] Azdel Slade: so rubaiyat, on the question of how much thing we do in sl "matter," do you think that the moves towards self-governance are like a prep for the future, or are significant to you today?

[16:07] Rubaiyat Shatner: our associations are real, and we are moving into new areas new forms of community

[16:07] Brianee Hoffnung: surely many people can rule our daily lives - if we agree - but if we try to transform our own daily lives?

[16:08] Rubaiyat Shatner: from that standpoint I think we are creating or have the potential to create the future of governance

[16:08] Azdel Slade: how? can you explain? it seems so much of governance relies on the promise of material security

[16:09] Brianee Hoffnung: it's kind of a razor's edge - you never really know if you are advancing or not

[16:09] Azdel Slade: oh, that was a q for james about the future of governance

[16:09] Rubaiyat Shatner: security in your "person"

[16:09] Azdel Slade: calder can u move back a bit?

[16:09] Rubaiyat Shatner: yes there is a sense of security that surrounds governance rather that we submit(?) ourselves to governance for the right to life, liberty and security of person

[16:10] YaoChi Zhangsun: and the concept of consent

[16:10] Feilen Timeless: So the point of governance is a balance between security and freedom

[16:10] Rubaiyat Shatner: exactly

[16:10] Azdel Slade: thx calder! sorry its so small in here, its a scale model of the real room, which is nice and big in real life - 17x30 but feels cramped in sl - or cozy rather

[16:11] Brianee Hoffnung: material security is going to be a bigger issue now - but precisely that will allow people to focus better on what is important

[16:11] Rubaiyat Shatner: Feilen there is something askew about that observation

[16:11] Feilen Timeless: X3 The screen doesn't really show how big it is as well - Ctrl+8,9,0 will adjust to feel right

[16:12] Azdel Slade: i bring it up beause of course with virtual worlds theres the question of escapism and ignoring material reality - for example, i read that the average sl avatar

[16:13] Symphony Delicioso: which does happen

[16:13] Azdel Slade: consumes more energy than the avg person in brazil - so experimenting here has its own cost, and perhaps at the detriment of other issues like ecology

[16:13] Brianee Hoffnung: now this is a question

[16:14] YaoChi Zhangsun: this may be viewed as a channel of resource consumption in some respects, but it is also a channel of creation.

[16:14] Brianee Hoffnung: why exactly did you choose this venue, micha?

[16:14] Azdel Slade: a few reasons

[16:14] jbird Huckleberry is Online

[16:14] Azdel Slade: one that the client is open source/free software means that we can, and did, change it to suit our needs, adding code

[16:15] echolalia Azalee is Online

[16:15] Azdel Slade: another is that i'm very interested in bringing together the body and technology
and avatars have a strong element of embodiment here

[16:16] Brianee Hoffnung: I'm feeling pretty disembodied!

[16:16] Azdel Slade: another was being inspired by other artists doing perforrmance art here, and other artists doing online performance

[16:16] jbird Huckleberry: sorry echolalia didn't mean to bump you

[16:16] Azdel Slade: right, but reembodied as well in that gamer girl avatar, no? you said sl challenged, referring to the feeling of it not working, of a body not doing what you want
in a way but i'm also interested, strongly, in challenging the notion of what is real and virtual

[16:17] Brianee Hoffnung: yeah, the glam girl was the least i could do!

[16:17] Azdel Slade: in blurring the line

[16:17] Brianee Hoffnung: when it comes to changing your sex, the words real and virtual start to have meanings

[16:18] Brianee Hoffnung: very intimate meanings where real and virtual can't be separated

[16:18] Azdel Slade: definitely i'm interested in this process of how we become something - how we become what we want to become - so starting with an idea or image and then making it "real" - the challenge of politics, no?

[16:19] Brianee Hoffnung: yeah!

[16:19] jbird Huckleberry: i think so, to reimagine our lives is very political

[16:19] Rubaiyat Shatner: micha how do you feel about your "presence" in SL, you you feel it merits rights or prepresents something other than your physical self?

[16:19] Brianee Hoffnung: but there ae many arenas for that challenge, no?

[16:19] Azdel Slade: first, james...yes, in as much as it is an extension of my own experience - in another discussion, we talked about the article "a rape in cyberspace"

[16:20] Brianee Hoffnung is Offline

[16:20] Azdel Slade: the the notion of mental and emotional harm

[16:20] Rubaiyat Shatner: yes I am familiar with that

[16:20] Azdel Slade: so surely, since i'm here experiencing this and experiencing it in a big way, with the visor and all

[16:20] IM: Feilen Timeless: Perfect for HMDs, Sl's FOV is ~80 degrees

[16:21] Azdel Slade: theres lots of possibility for harm

[16:21] Rubaiyat Shatner: we seem to be setting or rather acknowledging a heirarchy (pardon my spelling)

[16:21] IM: Feilen Timeless: Most HMD's are lower, it will feel more real if you limit it a bit

[16:21] jbird Huckleberry: images and embodied experience are deeply connected

[16:21] YaoChi Zhangsun: aren't we heirarchical beings ?

[16:21] Rubaiyat Shatner: well we certainly like to create or notice heirarchys

[16:22] Rubaiyat Shatner: so I have no question that if I were to be assaulted that would certainly take precidence

[16:23] Rubaiyat Shatner: but assuming I were reasonably secure in my physical being, is there something to be said for my emotional being in SL (or whever, chat room phone call, whatnot)

[16:23] Azdel Slade: sorry, adjusting hmd, feilen just gave me a great tip...

[16:24] YaoChi Zhangsun: wouldn't that depend on 1.) your emotional security and 2.) the consideration of others in SL with whom you are interacting ?

[16:24] Rubaiyat Shatner: is it biopolitics?

[16:24] Azdel Slade: well its also a question of the realism, i think

[16:24] YaoChi Zhangsun: I.E. how they treat you in terms of kindness or cruelty

[16:24] Azdel Slade: because going to an s&m dungeon in sl, is to me, mostly hilarious. because of the awkwardness of the graphics

[16:25] YaoChi Zhangsun: Folks sometimes expose their spirits in the virtual world. they can be injured emotionally

[16:25] Azdel Slade: but as with anything, as with text, you can imagine more if you want to

[16:25] Rubaiyat Shatner: see graphics are almost secondary, I have friends who were mudders who had compelling experiences in text

[16:25] YaoChi Zhangsun: Indeed

[16:25] Azdel Slade: yes, there was a good article in the book second person that partly inspired this project

[16:25] Feilen Timeless: The idea seems to focus around experimenting in something we do not have the chance to, or the ability to in real life

[16:25] YaoChi Zhangsun: But not just that.

[16:25] Nyx Linden: so it depends on the observer to make the determination - even in real life, people will have different emotional reactions to different situations

[16:25] YaoChi Zhangsun: Connecting to other people

[16:25] jbird Huckleberry: is it also an question of intentionality and consent?

[16:26] Azdel Slade: where numerous people said they felt "more like themselves" as their game characters than as their real life person

[16:26] YaoChi Zhangsun: In may respects, our interactions are quite real.

[16:26] Rubaiyat Shatner: is this "place" seperate from our bodies?

[16:26] Alynna Vixen: my spirit is certainly exposed here

[16:26] Feilen Timeless: Also in protecting one's identity and using the prefered one.

[16:26] Azdel Slade: which seemed to me to tie into the experience of trans people, feeling more like themselves as another gender

[16:26] YaoChi Zhangsun: Sometimes the 'preferred identity' is the one sheltered in the RL world. Sometimes that IS the vulnerable one

[16:26] Feilen Timeless: It just happens to be what you're embodying yourself as at the moment, whereas you can do the same in IRC as a name and a description

[16:27] Rubaiyat Shatner: well there are certainly elements of identity construction available here as everywhere

[16:27] Alynna Vixen: I feel that the me I am on SL is a more accurate representation of my true self than the one that I have in the 'real world'.

[16:27] Feilen Timeless: You can only see what the real person behind the eyes or in this case, the screen, by knowing or being that person - I share that notion

[16:27] Azdel Slade: so then, this ties back into biopolitics, into how much you can "be" what you want on a daily basis

[16:27] jbird Huckleberry: to have the space to express ourselves and our imaginations, its important. without the imagination to visualize and feel who and what we are then it seems we are more disconnected from our bodies then some to thier avatars

[16:28] Brianee Hoffnung: you all look great actually - I have just been taking time to look and enjoy

[16:28] Rubaiyat Shatner: I am wondering how a "place" like this can impact biopolitics

[16:28] Nyx Linden: what about the malleability of identity in virtual worlds such as this? Within a few seconds I can change my avatar, or expression of my identity, into something completely different. I could even sign into a different account and no one could tell I was the same person behind the computer.

[16:29] Azdel Slade: and thats part of what i'm exploring with my project, how we can use virtual worlds to learn a different way of living "in real life"

[16:29] Rubaiyat Shatner: Identity is not entirely about the skin

[16:29] Feilen Timeless: It's not a real place, but more theoretical, as in what we would be if this were really happening, which has just as much significance of if it really were

[16:29] jbird Huckleberry: do we not always hold multiple truths and identities?

[16:29] Feilen Timeless: It's only lacking true physical manifestation

[16:29] Alynna Vixen: in RL people would make assumptions about me, what was going on in my head and heart, based on my immediate appearance, assumptions that would be more wrong than right..

[16:29] Azdel Slade: wait, but feilen - it is real, we can see it and feel it

[16:29] Nyx Linden: (as a counterpoint most people who spend large amounts of time in SL tend to settle on a particular avatar or identity expression to use the majority of the time)

[16:29] Feilen Timeless: Indeed, and that is the definition of an experience

[16:30] Azdel Slade: and i agree with jbird, its complicated, we're never only in one reality

[16:30] Feilen Timeless: The significance is the same

[16:30] Rubaiyat Shatner: I have to agree this is real, it is not however material

[16:30] Brianee Hoffnung: it seems that or me to impact
biopolitics in this place I would have to go buy a big powerful
computer with a new chipset

[16:30] Azdel Slade: LOL - another problem, accessibility

[16:30] Rubaiyat Shatner: lol

[16:30] Feilen Timeless: It is real to the higher degree, as it
expresses what CAN happen, not mearly what could

[16:30] jbird Huckleberry: it can be material in our embodied
experiences and that we can learn from the virtual

[16:31] Feilen Timeless: What merely happens to be

[16:31] Azdel Slade: but one nice thing is that SL has users from
all over, i think only 45% or 50% are from the US even

[16:31] Rubaiyat Shatner: learning, imagination, communication

[16:31] YaoChi Zhangsun: Actaully even just literate access to
SL and the mere ability to realize influential posts in world
could have unexpected impacts

[16:31] Azdel Slade: I've met people in europe, asia, latin
america

[16:31] YaoChi Zhangsun: Thoughts and ideas can be viral

[16:31] Feilen Timeless: And above all, diversity

[16:31] Rubaiyat Shatner: how do they impact biopolitics?

[16:32] Alynna Vixen: i dont think that anyone can truly govern
themselves in this world until the simulator is under their own
roof, on a server that is irrevocable by any entity but the one(s)
governing the simulator(s) though.

[16:32] Nyx Linden: it could also be seen as a platform for connecting people from different regions and beliefs on biopolitics and what it should be, to enable the exchange of information in a richer context than just text

[16:32] Feilen Timeless: They can govern their actions, providing no one else is doing it for then

[16:32] Rubaiyat Shatner: you cannot govern yourself while you are beholden to a set of terms of service

[16:32] Feilen Timeless: *them

[16:32] Rubaiyat Shatner: esp when the ToS are written to cover corporate asses

[16:33] Azdel Slade: i totally agree with james and alynna

[16:33] YaoChi Zhangsun: You have some degree of self governance within the limits of outside forces

[16:33] Azdel Slade: which is why i think its so important to expand the number of servers running opensim

[16:33] jbird Huckleberry: heart you all, i have to go work at the shelter <3. its been my pleasure

[16:33] Rubaiyat Shatner: just like you can start your own country in a mall

[16:33] YaoChi Zhangsun: and for the open sim project to achieve more stability

[16:33] Rubaiyat Shatner: untill you get asked to leave

[16:33] Azdel Slade: bye jbird

[16:33] Rubaiyat Shatner: by jbird

[16:33] Azdel Slade: for example last night

[16:34] Feilen Timeless: Later!

[16:34] jbird Huckleberry is Offline

[16:34] Alynna Vixen: also, LL is not even equipped to deal with governance issues to cover their own TOS, neither are the tools given to allow self-government.

[16:34] Azdel Slade: my friends and i were having great fun vandalizing an air force base in sl

[16:34] YaoChi Zhangsun: Well, Rubaiyat, we get hit by griefers often enough. They get ejected and find their way back inside over and over again

[16:34] Azdel Slade: http://flickr.com/photos/azdelslade/3097816946/ but we knew that if we left it, they could just terminate our accounts and we could lose our inventories and everything...

[16:34] Rubaiyat Shatner: governance is ugly, time consuming

[16:34] Azdel Slade: so we have no rights at all, not to property or even existence here -for me, as an artist, it means that i'm probably never going to construct things in sl again as they can be taken away at any time. i would use opensim on my own computers

[16:35] Rubaiyat Shatner: you do NOT need your own servers

[16:35] Azdel Slade: the only thing sl offers is a public (which is significant)

[16:35] YaoChi Zhangsun: Even in the RL world our rights are prevented from contravention, by mutual understandings of where our rights start and end.

[16:35] Azdel Slade: why james?

[16:35] YaoChi Zhangsun: Else we would stamp all over one another's rights all the time

[16:36] Rubaiyat Shatner: unless by YOUR OWN you include a collective ownership of the "government"

[16:36] Brianee Hoffnung: how about Sharing is Sexy? did you (do you) feel sufficiently in control of that?

[16:36] YaoChi Zhangsun: Sociopaths are the ones who fail to respect the 'other' person's spaces and rights

[16:36] Azdel Slade: brian, yes

[16:36] Rubaiyat Shatner: SL offers population and limited IP

[16:36] Azdel Slade: because we pay for our own hosting

[16:36] Rubaiyat Shatner: which is great, I am truly a fan

[16:36] Azdel Slade: and have our own copies of everything

[16:36] YaoChi Zhangsun: But even a collective can be oppressive

[16:36] Azdel Slade: :-)

[16:36] YaoChi Zhangsun: A tyranny of the majority

[16:37] Feilen Timeless: In my opinion, the best governance is a Technocracy

[16:37] Nyx Linden: you pay who for your own hosting?

[16:37] Rubaiyat Shatner: yes and even a server needs a connection :)

[16:37] Azdel Slade: for sharing is sexy, another project i worked on - but honestly we dont admin the server

[16:37] YaoChi Zhangsun: Do you use Second Inventory ?

[16:37] Azdel Slade: we just installed the software

[16:37] YaoChi Zhangsun: to protect your assets from loss ?

[16:37] Azdel Slade: no, but thats a good point yaochi

[16:37] Rubaiyat Shatner: democracy is messy and drawn out and often just a pain

[16:37] Azdel Slade: i could and should

[16:38] Brianee Hoffnung: I like Rubaiyat's remarks on democracy

[16:38] Rubaiyat Shatner: I am really interested in the bio connection here

[16:38] Azdel Slade: yay productive meetings!

[16:38] Rubaiyat Shatner: because it is a point around which I am struggling

[16:38] Feilen Timeless: A technocracy is based on those of the highest relative intellegence, the scientists, instead of those elected

[16:38] Azdel Slade: i mean, productive encounters, not like collective meeting meetings, lol - what is, rubaiyat?

[16:39] Feilen Timeless: Relative intellegence being quickness of reasoning and learning, not education

[16:39] Rubaiyat Shatner: are we eligable for nation status? or are we locked in our bio physicality

[16:40] YaoChi Zhangsun: Well, we as intelligent beings have a strong tendency to set our paradigms and be extremely resistant to revising them later.

[16:40] Brianee Hoffnung: our virtual friend is rubaiyat! the one whos asking for national status!

[16:40] Rubaiyat Shatner: does the "place" of our conscience have any weight what so ever - and rubaiyat is part of my identity :)

[16:40] Feilen Timeless: Democracy is judgement of the opinions of others, a corrupt technocracy would run on things that are best to know, also an opinion. Ability to know would be the best judgement, as it is a judgement without opinion

[16:41] YaoChi Zhangsun: well, the seat of our consciousnes is subject to the maladies of the flesh and can be messed up thereby

[16:41] Rubaiyat Shatner: I am not a fan of meritocracies

[16:41] YaoChi Zhangsun: would you prefer a demeritocracy ?

[16:41] Rubaiyat Shatner: lol

[16:41] Azdel Slade: lol

[16:41] Nyx Linden: this has been great - very informative. Unfortunately I must be going. Thank you Azdel for setting this up.

[16:41] Feilen Timeless: X3

[16:41] Azdel Slade: thanks for coming nyx

[16:41] YaoChi Zhangsun: Bye Nyx

[16:41] Feilen Timeless: Cya

[16:41] Azdel Slade: howd u hear about it?

[16:42] echolalia Azalee: ciao

[16:42] Azdel Slade: but james, your question was really interesting

[16:42] Azdel Slade: does the place of our conscience have weight?

[16:42] echolalia Azalee is Offline

[16:42] Rubaiyat Shatner: so my body is in california

[16:42] Azdel Slade: do you mean that responsibility is somehow tied to phsical being?

[16:42] IM: Nyx Linden: it went on a few mailing lists around the lab, and I noticed your posts on SL-DEV and decided to drop by as I had some free time. Good luck with the rest of the project :)

[16:43] Rubaiyat Shatner: yes, and forgive my ignorance, but I am not sure biopolitics can go beyond my body

[16:43] YaoChi Zhangsun: theoretically speaking it does not, practically speaking it can be influenced - a chemical imbalance in the nervous system can result in schizophrenia

[16:44] Rubaiyat Shatner: brian summed it up nicely when he referred to being murdered by police, that is the obvious trump, isn't it?

[16:44] YaoChi Zhangsun: that severely impacts the ability to analyze situations as they play out.

[16:44] Brianee Hoffnung: the place of consciousness is both weightlessand very deeply tied to mortal flesh, imho - and it is very funny for me, the wordsmith, to be such a cripple when a poor computer blocks my writing and speech! mortal flesh itself is dependent on money and technology....

[16:44] YaoChi Zhangsun: physiology constantly impacts intellect

[16:45] Rubaiyat Shatner: but, honestly I feel your presence

[16:45] YaoChi Zhangsun: You need a dragon, Brianee - Dragon Naturally Speaking

[16:45] Azdel Slade: but rub (i'm shortening rubaiyat cuz its hard for me to type)...

[16:45] Rubaiyat Shatner: and when your hands "in world" go typey typey I anticipate...

[16:45] Azdel Slade: biopolitics definitely extends outside of your body - to relationships

[16:45] Feilen Timeless: The more direct you implement of speaking and your nervous system, the better the analysis will be

[16:45] Azdel Slade: agreements - collectivities - the line between your body and my body isn't so clear

[16:45] Brianee Hoffnung: agetting shot by a cop is the ultimate reminder of how much I need a dragon - a becoming dragon!

[16:45] Nix Stransky is Offline

[16:46] Azdel Slade: if we're talking about our ability to create the world we want

[16:46] Feilen Timeless: When one has one's mind directly linked to another, it becomes one mind.

[16:46] Azdel Slade: its not just about my body, but about my relations with others as well, or more so

[16:46] Brianee Hoffnung: we need friends to create the world we want

[16:46] Azdel Slade: totally

[16:46] Rubaiyat Shatner: aren't you talking about collective action though micha?

[16:46] YaoChi Zhangsun: Not entirely one mind Feilen, but a shared space between two minds

[16:46] Azdel Slade: or we're just creating the bedroom we want - hah, maybe thats what i'm doing irl - now - jk jk

[16:46] Feilen Timeless: We actually have two, well linked by a nervous cord, which allows one conciousness while the brain will actuall argue with itself

[16:46] YaoChi Zhangsun: What we are doing now, can in a sense be defined as a form of telepathy.

[16:47] Feilen Timeless: That's what you feel when you're indecisive

[16:47] YaoChi Zhangsun: Thoughts transferred from mind to mind via some pathway.

[16:47] Brianee Hoffnung: the essential is the friends, their feelings, the ways you exchange, the signals of whatever kind

[16:47] Feilen Timeless: What we are doing right now is in fact more or less being one mind discussing with itself

[16:47] Brianee Hoffnung: and I would say, the essential is also the fights with all these ruling powers....

[16:48] YaoChi Zhangsun: The interchange of ideas is dependent on the evolution of conventions of communication that both parts have some degree of agreement upon

[16:48] Feilen Timeless: Each peice of a nervous system is capable of being independent, while grouped together it becomes greater and greater

[16:49] Azdel Slade: whew i'm pooped! it must be lunch time...

[16:49] Feilen Timeless: It can also be so in computers, although we will have a while before they can work as a human mind

[16:49] Azdel Slade: my friend just went to go get some dragon food (aka indian curry and rice)

[16:49] Brianee Hoffnung is Offline

[16:49] Feilen Timeless: Fortunately the brain is terribly inneficient

[16:49] YaoChi Zhangsun: Mmmmm, curry !

[16:49] Brianee Hoffnung is Online

[16:49] Rubaiyat Shatner: my people also like curries

[16:50] Azdel Slade: lol

[16:50] Feilen Timeless: So as such, intellegent AI's have been invented on a more effecient, (not the same working however) system

[16:50] Azdel Slade: ok, how about this...brian, james, any last words on biopolitics and selfgovernance in sl?

[16:50] Feilen Timeless: Cleverbot (http://www.cleverbot.com) is a bot that collects how it should respond based on how others respond to it

[16:50] Azdel Slade: so folks who want it tidy can go? and folks who want to stay and chat can, all day...

[16:51] Brianee Hoffnung: Azdel, thanks very much for inviting me here - I want to wish you luck and a thousand lives in one - biopolitics is first of all transforming your own life

[16:51] Feilen Timeless: Responses aren't perfect, as it only responds to what you said last, not on the whole conversation

[16:51] Rubaiyat Shatner: I think this conversation has been very productive, and yes thanks for inviting me as well.

[16:51] Feilen Timeless: However it only uses the power of 1/16th of an insect's brain

[16:51] Azdel Slade: thanks a ton for coming, brian, i'm also a big fan of your writing - and thank you too james, you've really constributed a lot to making this possible, the whole space! and i hope we can all talk or collaborate or anything in the future again...

[16:52] Brianee Hoffnung: This SL experiment is another set of feelings and signals, interesting, playful, I hope to come back with better equipment and a wilder avatar to enjoy it more!

[16:52] Pyewacket Kazyanenko is Online

[16:52] Azdel Slade: great, do! and i'll give you fun stuff like snowball throwers and rockets to fly on and show you around. today is day 10 so i'll be here for about 6 more days :-)

[16:53] Brianee Hoffnung: ciao, see ya all at the border!

[16:54] YaoChi Zhangsun: Thanks Brian and Rubaiyat - fascinating panel

[16:54] Azdel Slade: ok - thanks yaochi, thanks for participating everyone - seems like chat is a more "democratic" way to do this anyway... hah

[16:55] Feilen Timeless: Say azdel, is your group for this event free to join or just for support?

[16:55] Azdel Slade: feilen, the sl group is free, its just to get announcements of events, there's another panel on friday

[16:56] Feilen Timeless: Oookay

[16:56] Azdel Slade: about otherkin, or transspecies

[16:56] Feilen Timeless: Have a party to go to then, what time SLT?

[16:56] Azdel Slade: feeling like you're deeply, truly "born as the wrong species" - 7pm

[16:56] Feilen Timeless: Hmm - I can understand the feeling

[16:57] Azdel Slade: hmm, who moved the starmap? thanks brian, byebye

 [16:57] Nearby Stars to 10 parsecs: removing stars

Source Code

The accelerometer glove worn by Elle Mehrmand in
virus.circus.probe activates a vibration motor worn against her
vagina with a strap-on harness according to the amount of thrust
she applies to the dildo in her hand. The code for the Lilypad
Arduino that controls the glove follows:

```
/*
 virus.circus.probe - erotic motion sensing glove -
 accelerometer to vibrator
 by micha cardenas y elle mehrmand

 based on ADXL3xx code.

 Reads an Analog Devices ADXL3xx accelerometer and
 communicates the
 acceleration to a lilypad vibe board.
 http://www.sparkfun.com/commerce/categories.php?c=80

 http://www.arduino.cc/en/Tutorial/ADXL3xx

 The circuit:
 analog 0: accelerometer self test
 analog 1: z-axis
 analog 2: y-axis
 analog 3: x-axis
 analog 4: ground
 analog 5: vcc

 created 2 Jul 2008
 by David A. Mellis
 modified 4 Sep 2010
 by Tom Igoe
 modified 16 Jan 2011

 This example code is in the public domain.

 */

// these constants describe the pins. They won't
change:
const int groundpin = 18;            // analog input
pin 4 -- ground
const int powerpin = 19;             // analog input
pin 5 -- voltage
const int xpin = A3;                 // x-axis of the
accelerometer
const int ypin = A2;                 // y-axis
const int zpin = A1;                 // z-axis (only
on 3-axis models)
```

```
int motoPin = 5;
/* connect your MOTOR to digital pin 5 */


void setup()
{
  // initialize the serial communications:
  Serial.begin(9600);

  // Provide ground and power by using the analog
inputs as normal
  // digital pins.  This makes it possible to directly
connect the
  // breakout board to the Arduino.  If you use the
normal 5V and
  // GND pins on the Arduino, you can remove these
lines.
  pinMode(groundpin, OUTPUT);
  pinMode(powerpin, OUTPUT);
  digitalWrite(groundpin, LOW);
  digitalWrite(powerpin, HIGH);

   pinMode(motoPin,OUTPUT);
 /* declare ledPin as an OUTPUT */
}

void loop(){
  // print the sensor values:
  Serial.print(analogRead(xpin));
  // print a tab between values:
  Serial.print("\t");
  Serial.print(analogRead(ypin));
  // print a tab between values:
  Serial.print("\t");
  Serial.print(analogRead(zpin));
  Serial.print("\t");
  Serial.print(analogRead(zpin) + analogRead(ypin) +
analogRead(xpin));

  int accelValue = abs(1500 - (analogRead(zpin) +
analogRead(ypin) + analogRead(xpin)));
  accelValue = map(accelValue, 0, 500, 0, 255);
  analogWrite(motoPin, accelValue);
  Serial.print(accelValue);
  Serial.println();
  // delay before next reading:
  delay(300);

  }
```

The following code is a patch for Second Life that reads from a local file and moves two objects in the virtual world of Second Life. Elle Mehrmand and myself have used this code with numerous scripts for different performances, including moving the avatars in *virus.circus.touch* and drawing a live heart rate graph in Second Life in *virus.circus.probe*. We use Pd as a bridge to read the data from analog sensors attached to the Arduino and write that to a local file and then we use the following code to read that local file and move objects in Second Life. The patch applies to llappviewer.cpp in the standard Second Life 2.0 codebase.

```
// virus.circus patch - bring in info from pd

if(mainLoopPasses > 0)
{
    LLFILE *pureDataFile;
    char    dataFromPd[30];
    //size_t charsRead;

    pureDataFile =
LLFile::fopen("/pureDataFile.txt", "r");

    mainLoopPasses++;

    if(pureDataFile != NULL)
    {

        if(fgets(dataFromPd, (size_t)30,
pureDataFile) && (lastPdVal != atoi(dataFromPd)) )
        {

            //data read successfully!

            //store pd val so we only send when
there's new data
            lastPdVal = atoi(dataFromPd);
```

```
                llinfos << "read from pd:" <<
dataFromPd << llendl;
                llinfos << "number of reads:" <<
readsFromPd << llendl;
                llinfos << "mainLoopPasses:" <<
mainLoopPasses << llendl;

                //try moving the object every time
we read

                //if(readsFromPd < 1)
                {
                    //readsFromPd++;
                    //totalPdVal += lastPdVal;
                }
                //else

                {
                    /*if(readsFromPd > 0)
                    {
                        avgPdVal = totalPdVal /
readsFromPd;

                    }*/

                    avgPdVal = lastPdVal;

                    float numFromPd = 256.818;

                    float numFromPdOrange =
256.018;

                    if(avgPdVal){

                        numFromPd += ((avgPdVal -
60) / 50); //lets not throw the object 100 meters
away...

                        numFromPdOrange -=
((avgPdVal - 60) / 50); //lets not throw the object
100 meters away...

                        llinfos << "avgPdVal:" <<
avgPdVal << llendl;
                        llinfos << "numFromPd:" <<
numFromPd << llendl;
                        llinfos << "(float)(avgPdVal
/ 8)" << (float)(avgPdVal / 8) << llendl;
                    }

                    //sdsu - graphingObject
```

```
                        LLViewerObject *objectFound =
gObjectList.findObject(LLUUID("83dd12bb-85e0-3ee9-
a889-fa23e356e8a2"));

                        if (objectFound)
                        {
                                LLVector3 objectPos =
objectFound->getPosition();
                                //objectPos[0] = 237.824;
                                //objectPos[1] = 205.686;
    //home y - 43.877;
                                objectPos[2] = numFromPd;
    //home z - 278.575;
                                objectFound-
>setPosition(objectPos);

                                LLViewerRegion*
current_region = objectFound->getRegion();

                                if (current_region && (!
gMessageSystem->isSendFull(NULL)))
                                {
                                        U32 update_type =
UPD_POSITION | UPD_ROTATION | UPD_LINKED_SETS;
                                        U32 *type32 = (U32
*)&update_type;

                                        U8 type = (U8)*type32;
                                        U8  data[256];
                                        S32 offset = 0;

                                        gMessageSystem-
>newMessage("MultipleObjectUpdate");
                                        gMessageSystem-
>nextBlockFast(_PREHASH_AgentData);
                                        gMessageSystem-
>addUUIDFast(_PREHASH_AgentID, gAgent.getID());
                                        gMessageSystem-
>addUUIDFast(_PREHASH_SessionID,
gAgent.getSessionID());
                                        gMessageSystem-
>nextBlockFast(_PREHASH_ObjectData);
                                        gMessageSystem-
>addU32Fast(_PREHASH_ObjectLocalID,   objectFound-
>getLocalID() );
                                        gMessageSystem-
>addU8Fast(_PREHASH_Type, type );


    htonmemcpy(&data[offset], &(objectFound-
>getPosition().mV), MVT_LLVector3, 12);
                                        offset += 12;
```

```
                                LLQuaternion quat =
objectFound->getRotation();
                                LLVector3 vec =
quat.packToVector3();

    htonmemcpy(&data[offset], &(vec.mV),
MVT_LLQuaternion, 12);
                                offset += 12;

                                gMessageSystem-
>addBinaryDataFast(_PREHASH_Data, data, offset);
                                gMessageSystem-
>sendReliable(current_region->getHost());
                                }

                                objectFound-
>setPositionAgent(objectPos);

                                LLDrawable* drawablep =
objectFound->mDrawable;
                                if (drawablep && drawablep-
>getVOVolume())
                                {

    gPipeline.markRebuild(drawablep,LLDrawable::REBUIL
D_VOLUME, TRUE);
                                drawablep->updateMove();

                                LLSpatialGroup* group =
drawablep->getSpatialGroup();
                                if (group)
                                {
                                    group->dirtyGeom();

    gPipeline.markRebuild(group, TRUE);
                                }

                            }
                        }


                        /* mmc - do it all again for
second object */


                        //odyssey - right


                        LLViewerObject
*objectFoundOrange = 0;
```

```
//gObjectList.findObject(LLUUID("3226e71c-d049-767d-
f056-e5858a269ec5"));


                              //new object for mcasd right
                              //LLViewerObject
*objectFoundOrange =
gObjectList.findObject(LLUUID("3ab7efc2-bcdc-3330-
bac4-f85434f39567"));


                              if (objectFoundOrange)
                              {
                              LLVector3 objectPos2 =
objectFoundOrange->getPosition();


                              objectPos2[0] = 237.824;
                              objectPos2[1] = 205.686;
    //home y - 43.877;
                              objectPos2[2] =
numFromPdOrange;

                              objectFoundOrange-
>setPosition(objectPos2);

                              LLViewerRegion*
current_region2 = objectFoundOrange->getRegion();

                              if (current_region2 && (!
gMessageSystem->isSendFull(NULL)))
                              {
                              U32 update_type2 =
UPD_POSITION | UPD_ROTATION | UPD_LINKED_SETS;
                              U32    *type322 = (U32
*)&update_type2;
                              U8 type2 = (U8)*type322;
                              U8 data2[256];
                              S32 offset2 = 0;

                              gMessageSystem-
>newMessage("MultipleObjectUpdate");
                              gMessageSystem-
>nextBlockFast(_PREHASH_AgentData);
                              gMessageSystem-
>addUUIDFast(_PREHASH_AgentID, gAgent.getID());
                              gMessageSystem-
>addUUIDFast(_PREHASH_SessionID,
gAgent.getSessionID());
```

```
                        gMessageSystem-
>nextBlockFast(_PREHASH_ObjectData);
                        gMessageSystem-
>addU32Fast(_PREHASH_ObjectLocalID,
    objectFoundOrange->getLocalID() );
                        gMessageSystem-
>addU8Fast(_PREHASH_Type, type2 );

                        htonmemcpy(&data2[offset2],
&(objectFoundOrange->getPosition().mV), MVT_LLVector3,
12);
                        offset2 += 12;
                        LLQuaternion quat2 =
objectFoundOrange->getRotation();
                        LLVector3 vec2 =
quat2.packToVector3();
                        htonmemcpy(&data2[offset2],
&(vec2.mV), MVT_LLQuaternion, 12);
                        offset2 += 12;

                        gMessageSystem-
>addBinaryDataFast(_PREHASH_Data, data2, offset2);

                        gMessageSystem-
>sendReliable(current_region2->getHost());
                        }

                        objectFoundOrange-
>setPositionAgent(objectPos2);

                        LLDrawable* drawablep2 =
objectFoundOrange->mDrawable;
                        if (drawablep2 && drawablep2-
>getVOVolume())
                        {
gPipeline.markRebuild(drawablep2,LLDrawable::REBUILD_V
OLUME, TRUE);
                        drawablep2->updateMove();

                        LLSpatialGroup* group2 =
drawablep2->getSpatialGroup();
                        if (group2)
                        {
                        group2->dirtyGeom();
                        gPipeline.markRebuild(group2,
TRUE);

                        }
                        }
```

```
                                        } // end if object-orange
found

                                        //only reset this after we've
moved the objects!
                                        mainLoopPasses = 0;
                                        readsFromPd = 0;
                                        totalPdVal = 0;

                                } //end else if mainLoopPasses < 30

                        } //if fgets

                        fclose(pureDataFile);

                } //if file opened

        }
        else {
            mainLoopPasses++;
        }

        //virus.circus patch - end
        /////////////////////////////////
```

The following Linden Scripting Language script was used for *Becoming Dragon*. It reads motion capture coordinates from a URL which points to an XML file and moves an object in Second Life to those coordinates. By then attaching the object to one's avatar, the avatar becomes animated in Second Life according to the motion captured location of the performer's real physical body.

```
integer in_world = 0;
key http_request_id;
float timer_secs = 1;
integer moving = 0;
integer moves = 0;
integer max_moves = 60;

//begin xml reading code

list markers;
```

```
parseElement(string line)
{
    if(line == "<markers>")
    {
        //llOwnerSay("markers line found, starting new
markers list");
        markers = [];
        return;
    }

    // determine type of element
    string element = llGetSubString(line, 0,
llSubStringIndex(line, " ") - 1);
    element = llToLower(element);

    // parse known elements

    parseMarkerElement(llGetSubString(line,
llStringLength(element) + 1, -1));
}


parseMarkerElement(string line) {

    //llOwnerSay("parsing line: "+line);

    if(line == "</markers>") return;

      // parse attribute name/value pairs
    list parts = llParseString2List(line, ["=\'", "\'
", "\'", ">", "<\/", "\'"], []);
    integer n = llGetListLength(parts);
    integer i;

    // set default values
    string position_x = "";
    string position_y = "";
    string position_z = "";
    string visibility = "";
    string marker_name = "";

    // loop through name/value pairs
    for(i = 0; i < n; i += 2)
    {
        // read name/value pair

        string name = llList2String(parts, i);
        name =
        name = llToLower(name);
        string value = llList2String(parts, i + 1);
```

```
            //find content of marker node, slightly
               hackish
            if(value == "marker") {
                value = name;
                name = "name";
            }


            // assign known values
            if(name == "position_x") position_x = value;
            if(name == "position_y") position_y = value;
            if(name == "position_z") position_z = value;
            if(name == "visibility") visibility = value;
            if(name == "name") marker_name = value;
        }

    // add new item
    if(visibility == "true")
    {

        markers += [marker_name];
        markers += [position_x];
        markers += [position_y];
        markers += [position_z];
    }
}

//end xml reading code


default {

    state_entry()  {

        if(in_world == 0)
        {
            llOwnerSay("Hi, I'm the new movement
object xml!");
            in_world = 1;
        }

        llSetStatus(STATUS_PHYSICS, TRUE);

    }


    http_response(key request_id, integer status, list
metadata, string body)        {
```

```
        //if ( moves < max_moves ) {

    list coords;

    //llOwnerSay("http response received...");

    if (request_id == http_request_id)  {

        //llSetText(body, <0,0,1>, 1);
        //llOwnerSay(body);

        // parse out xml elements
        //list lines = llParseString2List(body,
["/>","<", ">", "\n"], []);
        list lines = llParseString2List(body,
["\n"], []);

        // loop through elements
        integer n = llGetListLength(lines);
        integer i;
        for(i = 0; i < n; i++)
            parseElement(llList2String(lines, i));

        //llOwnerSay("markers: "+(string)markers);

        //move by offsets in html body
        //= llGetPos();

        vector position;
        vector offset;
        list thiscoord;

        if(llGetListLength(markers) > 2) {

            //llOwnerSay("using marker
"+llList2String(markers, 0) );

            //coords for scale copy of lab
            //offset.x = (llList2Float(markers,
1)/1000) + 183;
            //offset.y = (llList2Float(markers,
2)/1000) + 16;
            //offset.z = (llList2Float(markers,
3)/1000) + 33;

            //coords for skybox
            offset.x = 139 -
((llList2Float(markers, 1)/1000)*4);

            offset.y = ((llList2Float(markers,
2)/1000)*4) + 53;
```

```
                offset.z = ((llList2Float(markers,
3)/1000)*4) + 234.3;


                if(offset.x > 0 && offset.y > 0 &&
offset.z > 0)
                {
                    //llSetPos(offset);

                    llMoveToTarget(offset, 0.1);

                    //llOwnerSay("+++ Moving to
"+(string)offset.x+" , "+
                    // (string)offset.y+" , "+
                    // (string)offset.z);


     llSetText((string)offset.x+","+(string)offset.y+
","+(string)offset.z, <0,0,1>, 1);
                }

                //moves++;

            } //end if coords

        } //end if (request_id == http_request_id)

        // } else {   //end if moves < 5

        // llSetTimerEvent(0);
        // llOwnerSay("Newmove   : "+(string)moves+"
moves! Stopping movement.");
        // moving = 0;
        // moves = 0;
        //}


    }


    timer() {

        //llOwnerSay((string)timer_secs + " second
timer elapsed, sending http request...");
        http_request_id =
llHTTPRequest("http://yoururl.net/vicon.php", [], "");

    }
```

```
    touch_start(integer total_number) {


        if(moving == 0) {
            llSetTimerEvent(timer_secs);
            llOwnerSay("Touched! Timer starting.
sending http request...");
            http_request_id =
llHTTPRequest("http://yoururl.net/vicon.php", [], "");
            moving = 1;
        } else {
            llSetTimerEvent(0);
            llOwnerSay("Touched! Stopping movement.");
            moving = 0;
            moves = 0;
        }

    }


}
```

Bibliography

Alexander R. Galloway. "The Unworkable Interface." *New Literary History* 39, no. 4 (2008): 931-955.

Baines, Anthony. *Bagpipes*. Pitt Rivers Museum, 1979.

Baudrillard, Jean. *Simulacra and Simulation*. University of Michigan Press, 1995.

"Becoming Dragon, 3 Minute Documentation." *Vimeo*, accessed January 5, 2012, http://vimeo.com/3874238.

"Blast Theory | Ulrike and Eamon Compliant", accessed January 5, 2012.
http://www.blasttheory.co.uk/bt/work_ulrikeandeamon compliant.html.

Boellstorff, Tom. *Coming of Age in Second Life: An Anthropologist Explores the Virtually Human*. Princeton University Press, 2010.

Dominguez, Ricardo. "Particles of Interest: Tales from the Matter Market » Trans_patent: 5, 439,686", accessed January 5, 2012, http://bang.calit2.net/pitmm/?p=33.

El-Tayeb, Fatima. *European Others: Queering Ethnicity in Postnational Europe*. Univ Of Minnesota Press, 2011.

"Frederick P. Brooks, Jr.", n.d. http://www.cs.unc.edu/~brooks/.

Grosz, Elizabeth. *Time Travels: Feminism, Nature, Power*. Annotated edition. Duke University Press Books, 2005.

Halberstam, Judith, and Judith Halberstam. *In a Queer Time and Place: Transgender Bodies, Subcultural Lives*. New

York: New York University Press, 2005.

Haraway, Donna J. *When Species Meet*. Univ Of Minnesota
       Press, 2007.

Harrell, D. Fox. "CTheory.net", accessed January 5, 2012.
       http://www.ctheory.net/articles.aspx?id=610#_ednref32
       .

Harrigan, Pat, and Noah Wardrip-Fruin. *Second Person: Role-
       Playing and Story in Games and Playable Media*. The
       MIT Press, 2010.

"How Operation Payback Executes Its Attacks", accessed
       January 5, 2012. http://mashable.com/2010/12/09/how-
       operation-payback-executes-its-attacks/.

Lacan, Jacques. *Ecrits: A Selection*. W. W. Norton & Company,
       2004.

"Message to Anonymous - YouTube", accessed January 5, 2012.
       http://www.youtube.com/watch?v=_N3azFf6wiY.

"Message to Scientology - YouTube", accessed January 5,
       2012.
       http://www.youtube.com/watch?v=JCbKv9yiLiQ&feat
       ure=channel_video_title.

Munster, Anna. *Materializing New Media: Embodiment in
       Information Aesthetics*. Annotated edition. Dartmouth,
       2006.

Negarestani, Reza. *Cyclonopedia: Complicity with Anonymous
       Materials*. re.press, 2008.

"netwurker: [-eat-these-delicious-rebellion(_Lulz_B)oats-]",
       accessed January 5, 2012.

http://netwurker.livejournal.com/132340.html.

"Queer Technologies | zach blas", accessed January 5, 2012.
http://www.zachblas.info/projects/queer-technologies-2/.

"Re:Interview #005: Versatile m[c]o[mmunication]dality |
Mary-Anne Breeze | CONT3XT.NET", accessed
January 5, 2012. http://cont3xt.net/blog/?p=251.

"Ricardo Dominguez, Artist and Electronic Civil Disobedience
Pioneer: Gothamist", accessed January 5, 2012.
http://gothamist.com/2004/11/29/ricardo_dominguez_a
rtist_and_electronic_civil_disobedience_pioneer.php.

Rose, Chloe Brushwood, and Anna Camilleri. *Brazen Femme:
Queering Femininity*. Arsenal Pulp Press, 2003.

Salen, Katie, and Eric Zimmerman. *Rules of Play: Game Design
Fundamentals*. The MIT Press, 2004.

Shukaitis, Stevphen, David Graeber, Erika Biddle, and A. K.
Press. *Constituent imagination: militant
investigations//collective theorization*. AK Press, 2007.

Suskind, Ron. "Faith, Certainty and the Presidency of George
W. Bush." *The New York Times*, October 17, 2004, sec.
Magazine. Accessed January 5, 2012.
http://www.nytimes.com/2004/10/17/magazine/17BUS
H.html.

Szanto, Andras, and Orville Schell. *What Orwell Didn't Know:
Propaganda and the New Face of American Politics*.
Reprint. PublicAffairs, 2007.

"TransCoder | zach blas", accessed January 5, 2012.
http://www.zachblas.info/tag/transcoder/.

"Ulrike and Eamon. Compliant", accessed January 5, 2012.
http://www.dlwp.com/dlwpinternational/venice/index.html#.

"v.content", n.d. http://version.org/textuals/12.

"Virtual Sit-In in Solidarity with the Striking Students of
France! | post.thing.net", accessed January 5, 2012.
http://post.thing.net/node/767.

Warner, Michael. *Publics and Counterpublics*. Zone, 2005.

"Week 6 - Critical Code Studies Working Group", accessed
January 5, 2012.
http://critcode.ning.com/forum/topics/week-6.

"Who is Anonymous? - YouTube", accessed January 5, 2012.
http://www.youtube.com/watch?v=2K0E8sMDJ9M.

Zach Blas. "Queer Technologies." Accessed on January 9, 2012.
http://www.queertechnologies.info.

CPSIA information can be obtained
at www.ICGtesting.com
Printed in the USA
LVHW010042060221
678489LV00010B/836